An Anator

Amabel Williams-Ellis

Alpha Editions

This edition published in 2019

ISBN : 9789353808440

Design and Setting By
Alpha Editions
email - alphaedis@gmail.com

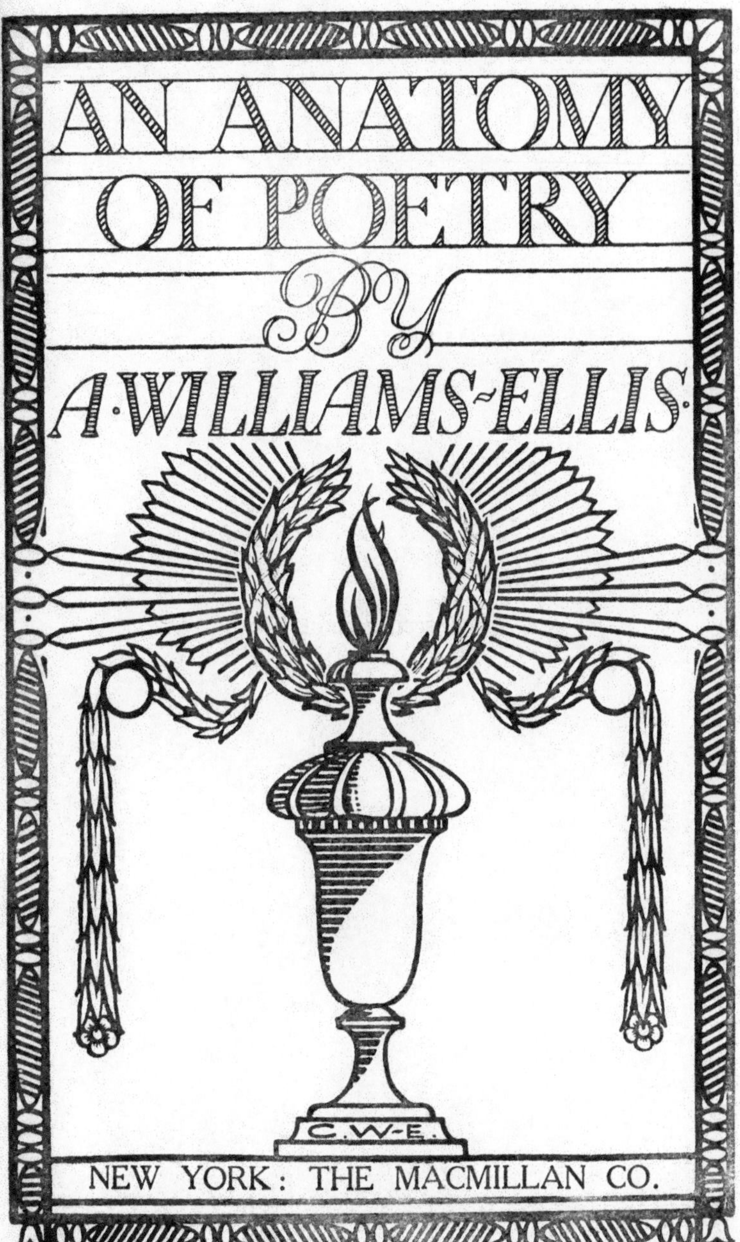
AN ANATOMY OF POETRY
BY
A·WILLIAMS-ELLIS
C.W-E.
NEW YORK: THE MACMILLAN CO.

PRINTED IN ENGLAND

CONTENTS

NOTE

Certain portions of this book have appeared from time to time in *The Spectator.*

The author acknowledges the courtesy of the authors and publishers in giving her permission to quote excerpts from the following books: A. D. Waley's *Japanese Poetry* (Milford) and *More Translations from the Chinese* (Allen and Unwin); Mr. Masefield's works (Heinemann); Charlotte Mew's *The Farmer's Bride* (Poetry Bookshop); E. V. Lucas's *Parodies Regained* (Methuen); Edward Shanks's *The Island of Youth* (Collins) and *The Queen of China* (Secker); Augustine Rivers's *The Death of Mercury* (Daniel); W. W. Gibson's works (MacMillan); Osbert Sitwell's *De Luxe* (Leonard Parsons); Rupert Brooke's *1914 and other Poems,* and Edmund Blunden's *Waggoner* (Sidgwick and Jackson); Robert Nicholls's *Aurelia* (Chatto and Windus); D. H. Lawrence's *Amores* (Duckworth); J. E. Flecker's *Collected Poems* (Secker); Sturge Moore's works (Grant Richards); Aldous Huxley's *Crome Yellow* (Chatto and Windus); and Walter de la Mare's *Collected Works* and *The Veil* (Constable).

A. W.-E.

JUNE, 1922.

PART I

(FOR ALL)

Chapter I

MODERN THOUGHT AND MODERN POETRY

I

Who was it who was inspecting a Board School and,—talking about Byron,—mentioned the word 'Athens?' He turned to the class of children, and said: 'Where is Athens?' There was dead silence. When he added impressively, 'This is geography,' a dozen hands at once went up.

In almost every field of knowledge people are at work now trying to bring about the end of what we may call the age of bulkheads. It was, of course, a tremendous advance when the bulkheads were set up, when in the seventeenth century, Philosophy, which had once stood for any sort of knowledge that was not divinity or history, began to be divided up into Natural Philosophy, Rhetoric, Grammar, Metaphysics, and so on. It was all gain when in 'natural philosophy,' Botany separated itself from Geology. But we have all felt lately that the time had come for the pendulum to swing back again. Knowledge was beginning to suffer from the fact that the man who studied cryptogams would hold firmly aloof from phanarogams. The supply of facts kept up, but we were beginning to lack a few fresh general principles. Moreover, as each scientist pushed along his particular line of enquiry, it began gradually to appear that knowledge, like art, was one. This seemed at first rather a shocking discovery. For as soon as he got to the higher regions of the conical hill of knowledge each scientist, however conscientious, observed that he seemed to be trespassing on somebody else's ground. Professor Einstein, Mr. Bertram Russell, Professor Whitehead, and Professor Keynes, for instance, a little while ago appeared to spend half their working lives in explaining how innocently they found themselves (*a*) poaching on each other's preserves, and (*b*) wandering on to the arch Tom-Tiddler's ground. Human psychology. And what is more, these gentlemen really were as innocent as babes, and had, as they averred, been landed in these questionable regions while each following perfectly legitimate lines of enquiry in their own subjects. It all came of the peculiar shape of the hill of knowledge.

At last it occurred to somebody to wonder if the overlapping of scientists might not be as harmless as the overlapping of tiles. Then it was that everybody suddenly found out what a fascinating game this synthesis was, and humble investigators on the lower slopes began to ape their betters. Captains of Industry began to study Psychology, Psychologists began to study Factories or Metaphysics, Metaphysicians began to study Astronomy, Astronomers learnt Logic and Psychology. And now the arts have been drawn into the vortex.

Psychologists and students of comparative religion have, of course, necessarily long concerned themselves with primitive art. At last we have all, poets, critics, and psychologists, begun to wonder whether a study of modern and civilised art, rather from the same point of view, might not yield interesting results.

Why do people paint pictures? Why do people buy pictures? Why do people write poetry? Why do people read poetry? They always have, and they apparently always mean to. How is aesthetic experience related to other experiences and to life in general? Is the poet a maker of beauty or a prophet of the laws? These are some of the questions that we have begun to ask ourselves,—to ask with a certain shame for they seem so indecently fundamental.

Now the modern poetic movement has been defined as being among other things a movement which is bringing poetry closer to everyday life. Here then is a sort of natural movement toward synthesis for us to study. Perhaps therefore before we try to consider the alarmingly large, vague question, 'What is poetry for?' we shall find it easier if we first ask the smaller question, 'What is modern poetry for?'

What shall we actually find if we look at the new poetic movement as contrasted with other poetic movements of other epochs? What is its nature and how does it function? If we try to study the relations between poetry and life as they exist at the moment, we at any rate find that we know something of one factor. We are all of us bound to have to some extent a first hand knowledge of what we mean when we say 'Modern Life.' It is for this reason that before attacking any of the fundamental questions of psychology and aesthetics, I first propose to consider the modern poetic movement and its antecedents.

At any rate I like to think that this is the reason. Perhaps the real reason is that the main question, 'What does poetry do, and how does it do it?' is so difficult that I prefer to conceal my attempt to deal with it in the comparative privacy of the middle of the book.

II

It is sometimes very difficult to be sure that there is such a thing as a homogeneous mass which we can conveniently call poetry in general.

What is curious about poetry is that rather more definitely than the other arts it laminates. It divides itself into strata corresponding with epochs. Really it is the epoch-made likeness between such pairs as Chaucer and Gower: Green and Webster: Crashaw and Donne: Pope and Young: Wordsworth and Coleridge: Tennyson and Browning, not their individual diversity, which is surprising. If we do not press the distinction too far, we can quite easily distinguish the verse of any age from that of any other age and, incidentally, modern verse from the verse of any other period whatever. It is in vain to plead that modern poetry has no definite characteristics, because of two facts. First, there certainly exist poems which are definitely non-modern. No critic, however inexperienced, could pick up new editions of *The Song of the Shirt*, *Enoch Arden*, or *The Highland Reaper* and take them to be modern poems. They might all have been written yesterday, of course, but obviously much verse produced at the moment is non-modern. Secondly, there exist poems—Flecker's 'Santoria,' Mr. Sassoon's 'Every One Singing,' Mr. Masefield's sonnet sequence from 'Enslaved,' Mr. Robert Graves's 'Blackhorse Lane'—which have something in them which makes it clearly impossible that they should have been produced in any literary period but the present.

The three poems that I have instanced as definitely non-modern are, of course, all drawn from the immediate past of poetry, but though it is conceivable that we might be deceived by a line or two from some individual poem by Donne or Marlowe or from one of Shakespeare's sonnets, we shall not really find any difficulty in distinguishing any complete non-modern poem even from examples of such modern verse as are either imitations or derive pretty directly from ancient originals.

If we can distinguish the characteristic verse of this age from the verse of any other age, then we have succeeded in dividing our subject-matter into two rough heaps. There is a heap of moderns and a heap of non-moderns. The heaps are adjacent, and there are poems from each which have slipped down, and these almost cover the debatable ground in the middle. In John Clare's, Donne's, Blake's, Mr. Freeman's, and Mr. Sturge Moore's poems we are conscious of this slipping tendency. But it is easy enough to find plenty of typical examples from either pile.

What shall we find if we examine a handful of specimens from the top of the modern heap, all poems, let us say, written since the war? To take the broadest characteristics first, we shall find that these poems are the expression of an attitude of mind which is strongly contrasted with that of the Victorians. These modern writers were, we are to remember, brought up in an atmosphere in which the validity of certain truths and the admirableness of certain virtues were assumed to be self-evident. Those who had the breeding of them taught them unquestioningly the value of such qualities as courage, discipline, patriotism, and the subordination of self to the good of the State. They lived to see these virtues, embodied in the Prussian citizen, produce the late war. Some of them are now maimed or blind. They thus learned pretty forcibly the horrors of a taken-for-granted morality.

They had been further brought up to a belief in the efficacy of certain literary doctrines. For instance, the suitability of certain poetic forms to the treatment of certain subjects; the suitability of a special sort of poetic diction or, alternatively, of 'dialect' to poetic subjects in general; the absolute fatality to the success of a poem of the presence of certain poetic solecisms (rhymes like ' morn ' and ' dawn,' for example). They lived to see these taken-for-granted poetic formulae produce—absolutely nothing. The late Victorian and Edwardian Muse was quite efficaciously buried beneath a vast heap of ' thou shalts ' and ' thou shalt nots.' She was scarcely able to emit a squeak. If moral right and wrong had been obscured by formulae, was it not possible that so had aesthetic right and wrong? Again they asked themselves, had the poetic canons which they found to be now accepted ruled all writers in the past? They read a few of the old examples of *vers libre*. They read poems like ' When that I was and a little tiny boy ' and felt inclined to doubt it. Anyhow, all this had to be very carefully investigated, and the age of the ' tradition of the elders ' carefully ascertained. It was thus in a spirit of conjecture, experiment and doubt that the new poetic age began. For the first time for fifty years poets—like other people—began to believe it was possible that their instinctively-held ideas might be mistaken ones, that it was just possible that the main canons of aesthetics and morality were not—as had been previously supposed—as plain as pike-staffs.

I do not, of course, mean that there was no whisper of this questioning spirit before the war or even that under the Tennyson oratorio the attentive might not discern the strains of an illusive little obligato by Matthew Arnold. Human events never happen with the diagrammatic clearness that I have suggested. Some Bernard Shaw or A. E.

Housman will always write without proper regard for our systems of chronology either in morals or aesthetics, but it is sometimes convenient for the sake of suggesting a point clearly, to regard as the causes of certain effects events which were in fact only their precipitants, or even merely circumstances that convinced a great number of people of the truth or utility of doctrines which a small number of people had long enunciated.

Chapter II

THE POET AS MORALIST

But the failure of any system of taken-for-granted morality which the War brought to light, had, of course, a much more direct result than that of merely making the younger poets reconsider their technical creeds. The ethical upheaval had the strongest possible direct influence upon modern verse. What was the old attitude? Milton set out 'to justify the ways of God to Man.' Tennyson was even surer about the facts of morality than he was about the facts of poetry, because, we should now say, he was a good poet and an amateur moralist. It is also arguable that the Byron-Baudelaire-Maupassant-Wilde type of poet was just as sure about moral principles as he, only that their assurance took them the other way; they praised the flowers of evil. Wilde might be said to be, therefore, as it were, the obverse of Tennyson. Each of them was quite sure of what was right and what was wrong, and therefore bandied about moral 'claptrap' with freedom and gusto. The difference between both of them and the modern poet is that he regards the facts of morality from the other end, not as things to be defended or attacked, but as things to be ascertained. Hence a great deal of the alleged impropriety and absorption in questions of sex of the modern poet. Hence also much of the realism of such writers as Mr. Masefield and Mr. Lascelles Abercrombie. Ugly facts of the material world, or of the poet's or his characters' natures, must not have a blind eye turned to them. If we never look at them, how can we know if they are good or bad? We should have only a tradition instead of evidence.

With many lapses because he is human, the modern poet desires to call nothing common or unclean, not even smug self-satisfaction. The one thing which he fears, to which he cannot avoid hostility, is the aforesaid 'claptrap,' for he is aware of the fearful efficacy with which talk disguises a man's notions—from himself as much as from the rest of the world. He is for the truth at all costs; and, as all modern poems are obviously not successes, he sometimes sacrifices the unity of a concept, the harmony of a phrase, or even his sense of humour to this hunger for exactness. Very often he will limit himself to a puritanical plainness of phrase. This is indeed a very marked characteristic of much modern work. I should like to give the reader two examples of the effects of these apparent verbal returns to nature. One is by Mr. Joseph Campbell, and one by Mr. D. H. Lawrence. The first shows the Puritanical method applied to the elegiac mood:

THE OLD WOMAN.

As a white candle
  In a holy place,
So is the beauty
  Of an agèd face.

As the spent radiance
  Of the winter sun,
So is a woman
  With her travail done.

Her brood gone from her,
  And her thoughts as still
As the waters
  Under a ruined mill.

Here again is verbal Puritanism applied to a mood of burning passion :

And if I never see her again?
I think, if they told me so,
I could convulse the heavens with my horror.
I think I could alter the frame of things in my agony.
I think I could break the system with my heart.
I think, in my convulsion, the skies would break.

Poetry has come back to what is something like a Wordsworthian care and meticulousness in the matter of language.

Wordsworth's confessed aim was 'to bring my language near to the real language of men.' The moderns are no more afraid than was Wordsworth of the type of criticism embodied in Dr. Johnson's famous lines which Wordsworth quotes in connexion with his own defence of simple language :—

'I put my hat upon my head
And walked into the Strand,
And there I met another man,
Whose hat was in his hand.'

They do fear—to quote Wordsworth again—'What is usually called poetic diction, a language differing materially from the real language of men *in any situation* . . . and characterised by various degrees of wanton deviation from good sense . . . With the progress of refinement this diction became more and more corrupt, thrusting out of sight the plain humanities of nature by a motley masquerade of tricks, quaintnesses, hieroglyphics, and enigmas.' He proceeds to give several instances of poetic diction, among them Prior's: 'Did sweeter sounds adorn my flowing tongue,' which that poet in a paraphrase substituted for: 'Though I speak with the tongues of men and of angels.' Again, there is, he says, the 'hubbub of words,' in which Dr. Johnson versified Proverbs—'Go to the ant, thou sluggard, consider her ways, and be wise: which having no guide, overseer, or ruler, provideth her meat in the summer, and gathereth her food in the harvest. How long wilt thou sleep, O sluggard? Wilt thou arise out of thy sleep? Yet a little sleep, a little slumber, a little folding of the hands to sleep. So shall thy poverty come as one that travaileth, and thy want as an armed man.'

'Turn on the prudent ant thy heedless eyes,
Observe her labours, sluggard, and be wise;
No stern command, no monitory voice,
Prescribes her duties, or directs her choice;
Yet, timely provident, she hastes away
To snatch the blessings of a plenteous day;
When fruitful summer loads the teeming plain,
She crops the harvest and she stores the grain.
How long shall sloth usurp thy useless hours,
Unnerve thy vigour, and enchain thy powers?
While artful shades thy downy couch inclose,
And soft solicitation courts repose,

Amidst the drowsy charms of dull delight,
Year chases year with unremitted flight,
Till Want now following, fraudulent and slow,
Shall spring to seize thee, like an ambushed foe.'

Wordsworth brought speech and verse together again after a separation of a hundred and fifty years, but, inevitably, they again diverged, and by 1860 the poets were at it again, having substituted the influence of 'Romance' for that of Cicero. In considering the modern and Wordsworthian revolts, we are to remember that Wordsworth was reacting from the late unworthy followers of Pope and Dryden, and that the moderns are on the rebound from a less nonsensical use of verbiage. Consequently they are able to allow gorgeousness of language its true place which Wordsworth could not. They, in fact, demand no more than that every word should be used with intention and a sense of its meaning, colour, and associations, and that words should not be slopped about.

This sounds very simple, and we might think that, whatever their practice, all poets in theory used words with a sort of double nicety, with regard to overt meaning and also to symbolic or associative meaning. That this is not the case can be proved by five minutes' perusal of such a book as Swinburne's *Poems and Ballads*, where the highest place is intentionally given to matters of rhythm and an extraordinary number of rhetorical syllables can be found—words whose everyday meaning is even slightly inappropriate. The poet hasn't bothered about this, but has relied entirely upon the music and colour of his words and the momentum of his metre. A modern writer will almost always handle his words with extreme respect, however great the levity with which he may confront his subject.

This desire for exactness and truth has another aesthetic effect. If the poem be a subjective one, it may lead the poet to what may seem to most readers a disagreeable or perhaps a boring degree of self-revelation. If it is objective, it will lead to great detachment. We do not, of course, mean to imply that the objective poem possesses detachment in contrast to the subjective one, for a moment's reflection will show that to write an extremely subjective poem demands an even higher degree of detachment than the complete suppression of self. Consider some of Mr. Aldous Huxley's subjective poems, one particularly in which he speaks with half-grim, half-humorous despair of the boring insistence of sex:—

> 'Love—was there no escape?
> Was it always there, always there,
> The same huge dominant shape,
> Like Windsor Castle leaning over the plain?'

Or, as an instance of the objective type, Mr. Blunden's poem, 'The Pike,' of which the following is the second half:—

> ' . . . . still as the dead
> The great pike lies, the murderous patriarch
> Watching the waterpit sheer-shelving dark,
> Where through the plash his lithe bright vassals thread.

'The rose-finned roach and bluish bream
And staring ruffe steal up the stream
Hard by their glutted tyrant, now
Still as a sunken bough.

'He on the sandbank lies,
Sunning himself long hours
With stony gorgon eyes:
Westward the hot sun lowers.

'Sudden the gray pike changes, and quivering poises for slaughter;
Intense terror wakens around him, the shoals scud awry, but there chances
A chub unsuspecting; the prowling fins quicken, in fury he lances;
And the miller that opens the hatch stands amazed at the whirl in the water.'

Or, if both types be sought from the same poet, Mr. Siegfried Sassoon's or Mr. W. J. Turner's work would afford them.

It will easily be seen how, under the influence of this desire to state facts rather than to draw conclusions, writers are led to an elusiveness and detachment which in unskilful hands becomes inhuman. Miss Charlotte Mew, for instance, has great qualities of restraint and intellectual grasp, but her work would be very much improved if she could be a little less just and indifferent. Not, of course, that modern poets never draw morals. They often do so in the heat of the moment, but never with the satisfaction of a Pope, a Dryden or a Milton.

A new 'Man of Ross' and a new 'The Hind and the Panther' are inconceivable. Mr. Ralph

Hodgson, preaching kindness to animals, is as near as we come to 'The Man of Ross,' and I can think of nothing better for an 'opposite number' for the religious teaching of 'The Hind and the Panther,' than Francis Thompson's 'The Hound of Heaven.' And this is neither, strictly speaking, a modern poem nor does it preach any but the universal doctrine of mysticism.

It might seem at first sight as though Mr. Masefield draws morals, and indeed so he does after a fashion, but if we examine them carefully, we shall not find that they are very explicit. Mr. Masefield is really moved only by the faith of Keats and Shelley, a mystic belief in Beauty, the Holy Grail of the poets. But this fact in itself well illustrates the balanced temper of the age, for one of the popular accusations levelled against his work is that it is unnecessarily ugly. So scrupulous is Mr. Masefield in stating the case against himself.

Chapter III

ANNO DOMINI AND THE EXOTIC

We saw in the last chapter how a desire for frankness and an open mind have lead the modern poet to treat a good many subjects which have either never before been treated in verse at all, or have not been so treated for a couple of centuries. To these factors also, of course, are due a good deal of what some people complain of as the exotic element in modern poetry. But, of course, some of this 'oddness' is due to actual facts of Anno Domini. In 1922 the poet finds that most of the obvious similes have been made, most of the clearly appropriate phrases coined and passed from hand to hand till they are too much effaced for the poet's treasury. This has bred a fastidiousness which, acting on different minds, has had opposite results. To find instances among some of the few long poems of to-day, its effect upon Mr. W. J. Turner in 'Paris and Helen,' upon Mr. Shanks in 'The Queen of China,' and 'The Island of Youth,' upon Mr. Squire in 'The Birds' and 'Rivers,' upon Mr. Sturge Moore in 'Danäe' has been to produce a certain charming attenuation and remoteness.

Let us try to imagine to ourselves a sort of synthetic Victorian poem which will have something in it of 'Maud,' of 'Two in a Gondola,' of 'Woke Hill,' of 'Christmas Rose,' of 'The Golden Market,' of 'Sonnets from the Portugese,' and the tradition both of 'Paradise Lost' and 'The Prelude.' Imagine this composite creature moving along in the middle of the road. Mr. Squire, Mr. Sturge Moore, Mr. Shanks and Mr. Turner were, in the poems we have cited, endeavouring to pass it on the right—that is to say, by means of greater elegance, by means of less obvious effects, by the avoidance of *clichés*, by being, as it were, more civilised. Mr. Masefield, on the other hand, in 'Reynard the Fox' and 'Dauber,' and Mr. Lascelles Abercrombie, in almost all his works, have tried to pass on the left; that is to say, they have tried to be more fundamental, stronger, to achieve more force and drive, to show beauty and idealism (if they show them at all) as rising not only from man's most elegant emotions, but from their most primitive passions. The many failures of the right-hand group suffer from anaemia; those of the left-hand group are only too full of blood,—of curses and 'thick ears.' The two following pieces of verse are, to my mind, successful examples respectively of the right and the left-hand groups. The first is from 'The Queen of China' and the other from a poem by Mr. Lascelles Abercrombie.

'Oh, woe, woe, woe on China. Now is all
The fabric of the high-arched kingdom gone
And the fair Provinces, the Mountain Province,
The Province of the Plain, the River Province,
The Border Countries and the teeming Port,
The Cities where the wise old Viceroys rule,
Shaking their honoured governmental heads . . .'

'A little brisk grey slattern of a woman,
Pattering along in her loose-heeled clogs,
Pusht the brass-barr'd door of a public house.
The spring went hard against her; hand and knee
Shoved their weak best. As the door poised ajar,
Hullabaloo of talking men burst out,
A pouring babble of inflamed palaver,
And over-riding it and shouted down
High words, jeering or downright, broken like
Crests that leap and stumble in rushing water.
Just as the door went wide and she stept in,
"She cannot do it!" one was balling out:
A glaring hulk of flesh with a bull's voice.
He finger'd with his neckerchief, and stretcht
His throat to ease the anger of dispute,
Then spat to put a full stop to the matter.

'The little woman waited, with one hand
Propping the door, and smiled at the loud man.
They saw her then; and the sight was enough
To gag the speech of every drinker there:
The din fell down like something chopt off short.
Blank they all wheel'd towards her, with their mouths
Still gaping as though full of voiceless words.
She let the door slam to; and all at ease,
Amused, her smile twinkling about her eyes,
Went forward: they made room for her quick enough.
Her chin just topt the counter: she gave in
Her bottle to the potboy, tuckt it back,
Full of bright tawny ale, under her arm,
Rapt down the coppers on the planisht zinc,
And turned: and no word spoken all the while.'

I think it is almost certain that to a great extent these opposite effects, or if you will affectations, of style, have sprung from a single cause; Anno Domini. If these poets had lived in the time of Chaucer, Gower, and Dunbar, they would probably have begun every poem, as did those writers, with an invocation to Spring :—

> ' In May as that Aurora did upspring
> With crystal eye chasing the cloudes' sable.'

And this with great satisfaction to themselves and their readers. It is, of course, perfectly untrue to say ' It is too late to be ambitious.' The Children of the Muses are a nomadic tribe and when they have exhausted the fertility of one region, it is easy for them to fold their tents and move on across what are, it seems, the endless tracts of human knowledge and conjecture. All those of a conservative turn of mind, those who are temperamentally inclined to regard the words ' fickleness ' and ' movement ' as synonyms must try to take into consideration the fact that there are more reasons for departure from the old ways than the one for which they are forever on the watch—Lack of respect for the Traditions of the Elders.

Chapter IV

THE NEW MOVEMENT AND NEW STANDARDS

I HAVE said that at the beginning of the modern poetic movement a good deal of hesitancy, of intellectual modesty, and of experimentalism was to be found in poetic technique. One month a poet would employ an elaborate rhyme scheme and throw about a profusion of brightly-coloured syllables; the next he would confine himself to words of one syllable and lines of one word. He would be minutely introspective and meticulously objective by turns. Mr. W. J. Turner began by writing obscure, difficult lyrics about paleolithic cave-men or the cave-man that lurks within us. Mr. Graves, to ease a war-harassed mind, wrote fantastic bucolic poëms. Mr. Robert Nichols, confronted by the war, showed, in spirit and technique, the journalistic reaction of the reporter; so did Mr. W. W. Gibson. The Sitwells (Messrs. Osbert and Sacheverell and Miss Edith) endeavoured, like Mr. Graves, to escape, but this time into an atmosphere of *commedia de arte.* But Mr. Turner's latest considerable piece of work is 'Paris and Helen,' a smooth classical narrative poem. Mr. Graves has lately tried to get back to the atmosphere of real life. Mr. Nichols' best work is now generally reflective and written in a flowing style, and Mr. Osbert Sitwell's output is often one of 'reasonable' poems. The new movement, now feeling more secure in the needlessness of worship, dares a glance at the merits of the more regular of its predecessors.

Psychologists tell us that love and hate, or blind reverence and violent self-assertion, are opposite manifestations of the same emotions. This is certainly true in the case of such group psychology as we encounter in the consideration of aesthetic movements. At first the poets of the new movement were, like the rest of the world, inclined to feel a strong love-hate emotion in regard to such writers as Tennyson, and to feel the obverse of the general reverential attitude in regard to his moral attitude and technical methods. Now that the exaggerated love and reverence have disappeared, so have the violent hate and self-assertion. For though the influence of these emotions on the new movement has been greatly exaggerated, they did exist, at least, in certain writers. For example, Mr. Ezra Pound, one of the brilliant but somewhat negative and sterile precursors of the modern movement, felt them overwhelmingly.

The new movement seems, in fact, in the last two years to have reached something of a state of equilibrium. There was a charming, invigorating freshness about the spring, and in some cases we may regret the 'early manner' of this or that writer. But on the whole the modern tradition has probably grown to a state more promising for the production of good work than it was, say in 1918 or 1919.

It is very difficult to say in what this state of equilibrium consists, or how the present varies from the earlier state of the poetic movement. The obvious thing would be to say that the new poets have become less extreme and that they now appreciate the value of '*centralness*.' This no doubt is in part true, but it is also probably true that our —the reader's—conception of the poetic 'centre' has slipped more than a little. For when we come to examine the facts, there are plenty of ultra-modern poems being written. Is it that the poets are more urbane, or that even the most timid of us have grown accustomed to them? At any rate, we believe that poets and critics have reached a stage in the movement where they have achieved the judgment of a modern poem on its merits.

We do not love or hate 'Wheels' or 'Coterie'; we distinguish between the bad and good poems which they contain. This is largely because the volume of modern verse now enables us to guess by a comparative process what the poet is trying to do, and to expect of a given poem only the particular qualities for which the poet has striven :—

> 'When they said, "Does it trot?"
> He said, "Certainly not,
> It's a Mopsican-Flopsican bear!"'

We no longer say: 'This poem is unlike "The Dream of Fair Women," therefore it is good' (or 'bad,' as the case may be). A poem may have noble qualities which, to pursue the analogy, are incompatible with trotting. This critics and fellow-poets recognize. The poet is now absolutely free to write 'Mopsican-Flopsican' poetry, but with this warning, that we know to what heights such a poem ought to rise. Being let off the trotting we expect of the creature performances of equal difficulty. We have, in fact, achieved pretty generally a new standard of criticism—flexible, liberal—well adapted to its purpose. Alas! that it must ossify like its unlamented predecessor, and, after strangling a few promising infants of the next, the unborn poet generation, be carted away amid public rejoicings.

Is there positively no cure for human fallibility? If not, let us at least not fall into the error of the Victorians who would honestly have declared that they suffered from no such malady.

PART II

(FOR PHILOSOPHERS)

'That's the test for the literary mind,' said Denis, 'the feeling of magic, the sense that words have power. . . . With language man created a whole new universe; what wonder if he loved words and attributed power to them! With fitted, harmonious words the magicians summoned rabbits out of empty hats and spirits from the elements. Their descendants, the literary men, still go on with the process, morticing their verbal formulas together, and before the power of the finished spell, trembling with delight and awe. Rabbits out of empty hats? No, their spells are more subtly powerful, for they evoke emotions out of empty minds. Formulated by their art, the most insipid statements become enormously significant. For example, I proffer the constatation, "Black ladders lack bladders." A self-evident truth, one on which it would not have been worth while to insist, had I chosen to formulate it in such words as *Les echelles noires manquent de vessie.* But since I put it as I do, "Black ladders lack bladders," it becomes, for all its self-evidence, significant, unforgettable, moving. The creation by word-power of something out of nothing—what is that but magic? And, I may add, what is that but literature? Half the world's greatest poetry is simply *Les echelles noires manquent de vessie,* translated into magic significance as "Black ladders lack bladders." and you can't appreciate words. I'm sorry for you.'

MR. ALDOUS HUXLEY.

CHAPTER V

THE FUNCTION OF THE ARTS

I

IT is very difficult to define a work of art, or to say that Pythagoras was labouring under a misunderstanding when he sacrificed a yoke of oxen to the Muses on working out the Forty-seventh Proposition. A fairly acceptable notion is that in creating a work of art we are trying to make something beautiful. This applied to the arts of literature would connote that we were not only trying to express a meaning, but that we were trying to express beauty as well. Or the emphasis might even be reversed and the artist might affirm that he was trying to create beauty and that the meaning—the overt content—of his work was only incidental to its beauty. But this contrasting of 'meaning' and beauty by no means covers the whole ground. There are many beautiful episodes in 'Macbeth,' but we do not feel that a statement that what Shakespeare was trying to express was the tragedy of the murdering of Duncan by the Thane of Cawdor and Lady Macbeth, plus beauty, would satisfactorily define the play.

We shall find that our definition will cover a much wider range of facts if we say that Art is the effort to express, alongside a rational meaning, something of those forces which lie in that great hinterland of consciousness, the inexpressible. It would be possible to treat the story of Macbeth (this has indeed been done on more than one occasion) scientifically as a psychological 'case,' but the appeal here is shifted from the reader's emotions to his intellect. The beauties of Shakespeare's treatment are, as it were, the feathers which wing the arrow of the tragedy till it is carried straight through the intellect into the substructure of our consciousness. In Macbeth's account of the murder—the speech which ends:

> 'I had most need of blessing
> But Amen stuck in my throat.'

we are moved and shaken in a way which would be beyond any intellectual statement of the dangers of Macbeth's position. The peculiar atmosphere which pervades the Courtyard Scene, and which closes in upon us as soon as Lady Macbeth strikes her signal on the bell, is one that cannot be produced except by means that we should all readily grant were artistic. A so-called plain statement of the facts would obviously fail to acquaint the reader with the outstanding fact—that is the peculiar emotional tension—which made Macbeth's act differ absolutely from murders like that of Hare and Burke.

Mme. Tamara Karsavina, in an interview with a reporter a year or so ago, put the case of the arts in a nutshell. The reporter asked her what she meant by a particular *pas seul* that she danced; to which she replied, 'But if I could tell you in a sentence, do you think I should take the very great trouble of dancing it? ' There are, of course, many other notions besides artistic ones; there are, for example, many scientific facts—chemical reactions, mathematical equations—which cannot be put into two words, but that is a different proposition; they could in time be explained to any sufficiently intelligent person. But if Mme. Karsavina had talked to the reporter for a month, she could not have put into so many words what she meant by her dance, for the meaning was, we may be sure, concerned with curves of motion—a flowing undulated movement constantly interrupted by an effect of rigidity, an impression perhaps of the balance of muscular force supporting a weight, succeeded by a pose expressing lassitude—a sort of liquification of the body,—staccato movements alternating with flowing legato ones. If dancing was barred, notions of this sort could only obviously have been expressed through some other aesthetic form. She might conceivably have written for that reporter a poem which, though of course not describing the dance, would have conveyed to him similar truths about form and motion. She might more easily have said what she meant on the piano, or have expressed it in the inter-actions of light and shade, voids and solids, tension and relaxation, of a picture or a building.

The fact that there are many things that cannot be dealt with by any sort of direct statement is again rather well illustrated in the domain of architecture. A working drawing, perfectly accurate in every detail, of an unfamiliar building will give even a trained architect very little idea of what the building looked like; whereas a charcoal sketch in perspective, in which perhaps all sorts of non-existent incidentals had been introduced—a floating cloud to cast an emphasising shadow, an imaginary tree, a group of onlookers to give the scale—will make a picture from which it is perfectly easy to gain a notion of the appearance of the building and the intentions of the architect. The fact is that communication between one human being and another ceases to be simple directly we go beyond the desire to impart to our neighbours the fact that we are experiencing such things as hunger, thirst, love or hate.

The most superficial study of metaphysics brings home to us the fact that every one of us is shut into his own private consciousness. None of my experiences can ever be exactly your experiences, for an experience is a compound made up of that which is perceived and certain qualities of the perceiver. This is, of course, perfectly obvious in the case of a colour-blind man and a man of normal vision seeing the same landscape. Or again, if two persons of different temperament chance to have shared an experience, to one it may prove a joke, to the other a tragedy. Let us, as an example, suppose D'Artagnan and William Cowper together in a street fight in which a man is killed. To one it would be a slightly exhilarating everyday affair, to the other a terrible spiritual experience.

All literature and a great many other 'non-productive' human activities can be likened to the efforts of a prisoner—shut into the cell of his separate consciousness—to communicate with his fellows. We have an instinct, as strong as it is sound, to share each other's experiences and to pool any knowledge that any of us may have gained. Though we are each thus separately confined, we are aware that we are so enclosed and we can allow for differences in the aspect of life as seen from another cell. The more sophisticated of us can even allow for the modifications in our own point of view in a given matter made by our own acknowledged opinions on similar affairs. For instance, I was the other day discussing the Gilbert and Sullivan Operas with a man who said that he was somehow rather hostile to them. He had tracked his hostility down to his dislike of Gilbert's attitude towards women. He is a strong feminist. Being now aware of the source of his prejudice, he is, of course, able to a great extent to discount it and give Gilbert the credit for jokes which do not amuse my friend because of his bias.

But there is a much more difficult problem. It would appear that our consciousness and its knowledge of our own motives very much resembles our ordinary sense perceptions. For example, let us take as an analogy our ordinary perception of sound. Our ears only give us knowledge of a comparatively short section out of the middle of an entire range of sounds. There are a great number of sound vibrations that are too deep in tone for us to hear, and there are a proportionate number that are too shrill. The world is certainly echoing with sounds that we cannot hear. We are in very much the same position in the matter of self-knowledge. We are constantly actuated in our conduct by motives which are not in the least clear to ourselves. Proverbial wisdom is well aware of this fact.

'I do not like thee, Dr. Fell,
The reason why I cannot tell,
But this I know, and know full well,
I do not like thee, Dr. Fell.'

We are reading, a vague sense of uneasiness and restlessness comes over us, but very likely except with the help of some outside agent, such as the clock, we cannot tell whether it is a change of author, or our lunch that we want. To take another very simple case, a young man may find in himself a sudden enthusiasm for a particular career, or a particular line of study, and be honestly unconscious that he is inspired neither by industry, nor a love of learning, but the hope that in the pursuit of this work or study he may constantly meet a particular young woman. Again we can probably many of us with an effort recall likes and dislikes founded on some incident of our childhood. Few of us, for example, can revisit the scenes of a happy childhood without a definite emotional recollection. The tree up which we climbed with the kitten and crowned him Duke of Catoria with oak leaves will, as long as we can remember the incident, never be quite a common tree to us. There are probably quite as many of those childish incidents that are still valid enough to be acted upon, but whose actual occurrence we have quite forgotten. Professor Freud would say that they were not forgotten, but repressed because they were unpleasant. Mr. Bertram Russell, bearing in mind the unpalatable theories of the Behaviourists, would tell us that they are unconscious because it was natural for all our impulses to be unconscious, and that it was only about certain very clear and obvious mental processes that we were able to reason at all. According to him the process would be that Man when he began to reason had caught himself performing some action and had then promptly begun to wonder why he was doing it. Sometimes he hit upon the right reason, sometimes upon a ludicrously wrong one. When in one case he hit upon the wrong reason, and in a second case proceeded to act rationally upon his assumptions, it becomes easier to understand the very curious embrolios into which Man's thinking and conduct have got him from time to time. Primitive society's marvellously effective mutual arrangements for the cutting of throats and the general making of life intolerable,—becomes, so regarded,—a little less amazing. But whether we hold Professor Freud's doctrine of the suppressed subconsciousness or prefer the theory of the ocean of subconscious action out of which Man has managed to rear little islands of consciousness, or whether glancing at the experiences of our friends and our own conduct and the history of mankind, we merely conclude generally that man is a very odd and a far from rational creature, we must come to the conclusion that for each person there is a region of being—a spring of conduct, which is doubly hidden away. Our brother's conscious experiences are hidden from us, how much more his subconscious experiences, which in the natural course of things are hidden even from himself?

Human converse and the whole body of literature and science are concerned to speak across the first barrier. It is a more especial function of the arts—painting, music, sculpture, architecture, poetry—to deal with the obscure but potent forces that lie behind the second :—

> 'Fallings from us, vanishings;
> Blank misgivings of a creature
> Moving about in worlds not realised.'

As to which of the Arts fulfils this function most successfully, or, as we have been accustomed to say, which Art is the 'best' there has been never-ending, but I am inclined to think quite needless discussion. There is no more a stock 'best art' than there is a stock 'best' human being. Your consciousness and subconsciousness may be best approached visually, the next man's through the ear, and mine by the most intangible way of all—the way of literary art in general and of poetry in paricular.

Every poet and every critic is agreed that the emotions are especially the province of poetry. Now the emotions would seem to be in a special degree psychological amphibians, sometimes moving, that is to say, on the plane of the conscious, sometimes on the plane of the unconscious. Beauty, love, hate, anger, pity, and terror, are the devices we use in poetry. They are not only the subject matters of poetry, but are also its instruments. The double function fulfilled by beauty and emotion has led to a great deal of confusion of thought. Round this question, whether the beauty of a poem was its aim and end or a means to some ulterior aim or end, and, if so, what the ulterior aim or end might be, has centred a great deal of circular thinking. 'Beauty' and 'Rapture' are like the little steering propeller on an aerial bomb—at once a means of directing the missile and itself part of what is projected. Or if the reader prefers a more traditional metaphor, the poet's thought becomes through beauty and rapture like a feathered arrow which is able to transfix at once the intellect, the emotions, and the deeper consciousness which lies below these regions.

II

The need for expresson is so implanted in our nature that the reader has probably hardly put to himself what might be supposed to be the natural question, 'Why all this fuss about expression, why should (as you and the psychologist seem to put it) "Deep call unto deep" in this gratuitous way?' The answer is that we are gregarious creatures, and this deep-seated desire for expression is in itself a non-conscious piece of reasoning. There is something horrible to the human mind in the idea of complete loneliness and solitude. The desire for companionship has the compulsive strength of a biological necessity.

As Mr. Harold Child somewhere very justly says, a man who had grown up alone on a desert island could have extraordinarily little knowledge of himself, for he would possess no standard of comparison. In comparison and the subsequent ranging of opinions or events into categories, lies, the metaphysicians tell us, the entire and only method by which man acquires knowledge. You cannot have a category of one, you cannot compare unity. The man on the desert island, however ingeniously introspective, could only compare his reactions on Tuesday with his reactions on Monday, and know that on one day he was good humoured, but on the next took a pessimistic view of things. This would obviously not take him very far. A man's method of finding out about himself is in fact to discover that he is cleverer than Jones, but not so clever as Smith, lazier than Robinson, but a better walker than Snooks, better at dominoes than Brown, though Green is cleverer when it comes to Bradshaw. And so on, till we come to consider the most subtle attributes of mind and character. Not only does each generation, by means of books and tradition, to some extent, stand on the shoulders, or, at least, the toes of the generation that comes behind it; it learns through contemporary minds. The world is like the laboratory of some great scientist, whose ten pupils each experiment for a year along converging lines, each with special aptitude or special knowledge, each contributing a factor to the discovery of some scientific law which would have taken any one of them at least ten years to work out alone. Each of them is thus able, because he can communicate with his fellows, to add to his mind the complete piece of knowledge; he gets the result of ten years' work at the price of one year's work. If our minds are to fulfil their powers of growth it must, we realise, be through co-operation with other minds. Not only is there this individual need to be satisfied, but we all instinctively feel both edges of the proverb, 'Tous comprendre, c'est tous pardonner.' We have the double feeling that our profound ignorance of each other is dangerous. 'Will he understand my motives?' asks Timidity, on the one hand, and, on the other, Suspicion, 'What does the man mean by all this?' The shrewdest and most practical people, people who have as little love as is possible in any human being of abstract knowledge, will almost always admit that as a means to success, or, as a recreation, their one study is Human Nature. In order that they may not be misunderstood, and in order that they may understand it is absolutely necessary for them to have some idea of how other men's minds work. In a comparatively primitive state of society some such study is necessary to an individual in order that the other man may not fly at his throat. In civilised society where our relations with our fellows become more and more subtle, and as we come to deal with more and more complicated ideas, we more and more feel the necessity of understanding our fellows and ourselves as well as we can. We begin to feel subconsciously uneasy at the idea of all this loose dynamite, this uncomprehended human nature —our own and other people's—which lies scattered about the world ready to be ignited. We probably read the works of a poet for our pleasure in the beauty or the emotion that he gives us, and we shall probably never be reduced consciously to reading his works in order to gain some light upon our own or other people's motives. But I believe a great deal of our pleasure in poetry really comes from this source. A very simple phenomenon has probably puzzled most of us at one time or another. Why is it that we apparently experience the same little shock of pleasure in reading a beautiful poem, or learning a scientific fact? Probably to a great extent because the two things are the same. In acquiring the fact and in reading the poem, we are conscious of a little increment of power to ourselves. The beauty of the poem has revealed something to us, we are conscious probably only of the beauty, the revelation perhaps never reaches the reasoning plane at all, it is something quite intangible. We should describe it (if we were not checked for a moment by the paradox that it has perhaps come to us through a poem), as 'something that you cannot put into words.'

Let him who feels that all this talk of understanding, this stressing of the notion of communication is gratuitous nonsense, remember that the reasons for a number of grave industrial disputes, a quantity of divorces, and the late War are still matters of debate and conjecture. Suppose that to understand everything were in fact the ending of hatred?

CHAPTER VI

THE POETIC METHOD

THAT the functions I have tried to outline in the last chapter are in fact those which we do demand that poetry shall fulfil, is I think borne out by our dissatisfaction with a great deal of what we are compelled to admit is very good verse. It is the vague uneasiness which objects to, say, Pope's 'Characters of Women,' and feels that this is not really poetry at all. And if this expressing of the inexpressible is indeed one of the chief functions of poetry, we have to admit that Pope's Epistle hardly fulfils these functions at all, but remains as clear and logical as prose. It has only one thing in common with 'real poetry,' its great compression. Compression is, I believe, one of the expedients by which poetry is enabled to fulfil its special function. One of the technical characteristics of poetry and music is obviously that the whole work of art is not presented to the mind in an instant. In this they differ from the figurative arts, we take in the main lines of statue, building, or picture, in a single *coup d'oeil.* Music, drama, poetry, narrative, and the dance are all what we might call progressive arts; we may sometimes speak in a picture of certain effects leading up to certain other effects, but what we really mean is only that certain expedients are used to lend force and emphasis to the elements of the composition upon which the artist desires that we should concentrate. But in the progressive arts we may have a genuine leading-up. The whole is a succession of parts, and it is easy to see that the rate at which these parts are presented to us may make all the difference to our perception of them. An incompetent executant, who, unable to deal with a chord in a piece of music, plays it note by note, is not playing the chord at all, but something different. The superimposing of one sound upon another gives us a whole that is different from and has an existence independent of the parts from which it is made up. Now a use of words in a state as it were of compression, so that this choral or super-imposed effect is produced, is one of the devices by which very special effects are made in poetry. In prose the interposition of the smaller parts of speech between the main words produces what, to pursue our musical analogy, is something like an arpeggio. Mr. Roxburgh in his essay, 'The Poetic Procession,' points out how remarkable is the effect of the compression in Keats's 'Ode to a Nightingale.'

> 'O for a draught of vintage! that hath been
> Cooled a long age in the deep-delved earth,
> Tasting of Flora and the country green,
> Dance, and Provençal song, and sunburnt mirth!
>
> 'O for a beaker full of the warm South,
> Full of the true, the blushful Hippocrene,
> With beaded bubbles winking at the brim
> And purple-stained mouth;
> That I might drink and leave the world unseen,
> And with thee fade into the forest dim . . .'

Mr. Roxburgh adds that he tried to translate this to a clever Frenchman who could make nothing of it. 'How could wine taste of mirth,' he said, 'and how could mirth be sunburnt?' Mr. Roxburgh had necessarily played the passage to him in arpeggio, and the effect was perfectly different.

In prose the passage would have to go something like this :—

> 'A stoop of wine. Calling up a white sunlight, a grey powder of dust on the leaves of vines and olives on the hillside.
>
> 'Very cool it would be that Provençal wine, in a *chianti* flask, perhaps, or an earthenware pitcher, that had been buried in the earth, the digging spade you fancy, buried to half its length. O for a draught of such a vintage! It would taste of flowers; there would be an aroma of the green country about it—nympths, the dance under the trees in the evening after the warm Southern day, something of the songs of Provençe about it. Is not the wine the work of such sun-burnt merry-makers? Indeed, such a beaker would be full, not of wine, but of the very spirit of the South itself; the wine, the true ruby Hippocrene, and at the brim of the cup there would be winking bubbles, pale sky-reflecting beads on the flush of the wine, that should presently stain the mouth of the drinker. And so I would drink, and so I would leave the world unseen and like thee, O Unseen Nightingale, fade into the dimness of the forest.'

The reader will notice that with my prose, not only does he miss the metre, but the total effect of the passage is one of wordiness and dilution. And with all this lost, he will feel that the thing is after all only a bastard poetic sort of prose.

Miss Amy Lowell, that diligent experimenter, has endeavoured to get extreme compression into words arranged in a prose rhythm. Take this passage from the voyage to Japan of the paddle-steamer 'Mississippi :—

> 'Break out her sails, quartermasters, the wind will carry her faster than she can steam, for the trades have her now, and are whipping her along in fine clipper style. Key-guns, your muzzles shine like basalt above the tumbling waves. Polished basalt cameoed upon malachite. Yankee-doodle-dandy! A fine upstanding ship, clouded with canvas, slipping along like a trotting filly out of the Commodore's own stables. White sails and sailors, blue-coated officers, and red in a star sparked through the claret decanter on the Commodore's luncheon table.'

The net result of this sort of treatment is that most of the book, 'Can Grande's Castle,' looks like prose, but the whole of it reads like poetry. Note again the effects of compression in a very different poem :—

> 'Flavia's a wit has too much sense to pray
> To toast "our wants and wishes!" is her way.
> Nor asks of God but of her stars to give
> That greatest blessing "While we live, to live."
> Then all for Death, that opiate of the soul,
> Lucretia's dagger, Rosamunda's bowl.
> Ah! what could cause such impotence of mind,
> A spark too fickle, or a spouse too kind?'

This is one of poetry's indirect devices—and among the rest are periodicity, rhythms, rhymes, symbolism, and a particular employment of word association. Mr. Robert Graves, in his book on criticism, has worked out the theory of what he calls 'the incantational aspect of poetry' very completely. Just as the rhythmic song, dance and gesture of the witches' celebration were intended to induce a hypnotic state in participants and audience, so the rhythms or repetitions of a poem are used by the poet to soothe himself and his reader into a receptive condition, a state in which it is possible to get through the purely intellectual reasoning layer of our minds to its deeper tissues. It will be realised how important this periodic or incantational element in poetry has always been deemed, when we consider the amount of time and learning that have been expended on the study of metres and rhyme schemes and the whole stock-in-trade of prosody. So important in fact was this side of poetry felt to be, that a good many people have run away with the idea that this was poetry, and that the art of poetry lay in fitting some sort of meaning to a rhyme scheme.

As for symbolism and word association, association as well as the effects of a marked rhythm and repetition is very well illustrated by a poem which is also an incantation :—

THIRD WITCH : 'Scale of dragon, tooth of wolf,
Witches' mummy, maw and gulf
Of the ravin'd salt-sea shark,
Root of hemlock digg'd i' the dark,
Liver of blaspheming Jew,
Gall of goat, and slips of yew
Silvered in the moon's eclipse,
Nose of Turk and Tartar's lips,
Finger of birth-strangled babe

Ditch-delivered by a drab,
Make the gruel thick and slab:
Add thereto a tiger's chaudron,
For the ingredients of our cauldron.
ALL: Double, double toil and trouble;
Fire burn and cauldron bubble.
SECOND WITCH: Cool it with a baboon's blood,
Then the charm is firm and good.'

These notions are not so much horrible in themselves, as horrible because we, or rather the Elizabethan audience for whom the charm was intended associated each item in the stew with the most awful malpractices of which they could conceive.

There is, of course, a more subtle aspect of word association. It is among other things the moss which is gathered by the word-stone as it rolls down the ages, and a further discussion of association in this aspect will be found in Chapter VIII.

Lastly, I spoke of symbolism. One of Mr. Graves' own poems, 'The Sewing Basket,' is a very good and simple instance of a poem in which the overt content is loosely used to convey secondary ideas:—

THE SEWING BASKET.

(*A wedding present from Jenny Nicholson to Winifred Roberts*).

To Winifred
The day she's wed
(Having no gold) I send instead
This sewing basket,
And lovingly

Demand that she,
If ever wanting help from me,
Will surely ask it
Which being gravely said,
Now to go straight ahead
With the cutting of string,
An unwrapping of paper,
The airs of a draper,
To review
And search this basket through.

Here's one place full
Of coloured wool
And various yarn
With which to darn,
I've worked for you
Lettered from A to Z,
The text of which
In small cross-stitch
Is LOVE TO WINIFRED.

Here's a rag-doll wherein
To thrust the casual pin.
His name is Benjamin
For his ingenuous face;
Be sure I've not forgotten
Black thread or crochet cotton;
While Brussels lace
Has found a place
Behind the needle-case.
(But the case for the scissors?
Empty, as you see,
Love must not be sundered
Between you and me.)

Winifred Roberts,
Think of me, do,
When the friends I am sending
Are working for you.

The song of the thimble
Is, 'O forget me not.'
Says the tape-measure,
'Absent, but never forgot . . .'

If we do not try to read too much into the poem its meaning is, of course, perfectly clear and obvious. There is a double meaning, and two concurrent means of expression. Mr. Graves has amused himself with the use of the things in the basket as messengers and with a study of a feminine mind embarked on a piece of phantasy. It will be seen that in this double thread is a method of conveying notions almost entirely peculiar to poetry. Sometimes the poet gives us what we might call the prose as well as the poetic version of his thought. It would be difficult to find a better example of this treatment than the first and last verses of Herrick's most famous lyric :—

'Gather ye rose-buds while ye may,
Old Time is still a-flying;
And this same flower that smiles to-day,
To-morrow will be dying . . . .

Then be not coy, but use your time;
And while ye may, go marry;
For having lost but once your prime,
Ye may for ever tarry.'

Neither the language nor thought are here very profound, but their simplicity at least serves to increase their clarity. The reader will see how almost absurdly the direct statement narrows the meaning of the first indirect one.

Chapter VII.

THE 'ART FOR ART'S SAKE' DILEMMA.

Ruskin, Tennyson, Swinburne, Rossetti, and Stevenson were all of them in their several ways deeply affected by a controversy which came to be known as the 'Art for Art's Sake' question. Was an artist to be, as Stevenson, for example, held, a maker of beautiful things and to follow beauty wherever or into whatsoever company it might lead him? Or was he, as Tennyson affirmed, to be the noble teacher who should inspire the citizen and help struggling humanity on its way?

Almost every writer for half a century took sides upon this question, and the work of many of them was profoundly affected by their conscious attitude upon it—the decorative painters, the decorative writers on the one hand, and Tennyson and his like thinkers, who still would 'Justify the ways of God to man,' on the other. And now apparently the years have brushed the question aside. In all our modern criticism, in all the many diverse aesthetic creeds that are set forth, it finds no place. Which way has it been settled then? Is the poet to be Sheherazada, the amiable and ingenious narrator of the Arabian Nights, or a seer and prophet who is to lead mankind along the right road? This question seems at first a difficult one, as it is so abundantly obvious that no sort of tacit assent has been given to either proposition. How, then, has the problem for the moment solved itself? Yet, I think we shall find that it really has solved itself, and that in a not unusual way. We have shifted unconsciously on to another plane of thought about the arts and the ethics which belong to them.

Behind the 'Art for Art's Sake' controversy was, I believe, a tacit assumption that we all, the poet included, knew instinctively in any given instance what was right and what was wrong. 'Be good, sweet maid, and let who will be clever' was the *reductio ad absurdum* of this point of view. It was in vain for Stevenson to say that honesty was not as easy as blindman's-buff. His hearers interpreted this, I fancy, as meaning that the flesh was weak, not that the understanding was dim.

But we have gradually come to realize—some of us only gropingly on the unconscious plane, that there is some sort of catch here. Sir Thomas More believed unhesitatingly in the rightness of burning heretics. A fellow-don, in urging compulsory chapels upon Jowett, said, to clinch the argument, 'Well, Mr. Jowett, as far as I can see, it is a choice between a compulsory religion and no religion at all'; to which Jowett gave his celebrated reply, 'My mind is not of sufficient subtlety to distinguish between two such alternatives.'

The reader will easily recall for himself a dozen instances of what we might call the changeability of morals, or rather of the necessary evolution of our outlook upon morals. We have at last a long enough history behind us to realise that, though there may be the Platonic Ideas—the sealed patterns—of Truth, Honesty, Right and Wrong laid up in Heaven, their manifestations compounded with the shifting stuff of human life are very variable. Something of this truth is popularly expressed in the colloquialism that the old people acted 'according to their lights,' and this is where we have begun subconsciously to feel that the poet comes in. His work is to increase the illuminating power of the said 'lights.' We dare not say offhand, any more than can a judge who has not heard the evidence, what is right or what is wrong in a given case. Who knows, we may all at this moment in some matter—sexual morality, perhaps—be acting upon ethical principles as mistaken as were those of the heretic burners, who were often, like Sir Thomas More, the most conscientious of men, acting from the sternest sense of duty. Such or such a line of conduct is accused of being wrong; the man who would stop the poet or the writer from defending the accused line of conduct is acting in the spirit of a judge who refuses to hear the counsel for the defence. The analogy between the function of a poet, or at least one of his functions, and that of the advocate is a very close one. If the poet, by taking thought or by inspiration, is visited with a gleam of understanding of the motives of some other human being in performing a certain action, he is very much in the position of the briefed advocate. It is his business to put the point of view up for what it is worth. This was a matter which

Browning thoroughly understood. Take for example 'The Statue and the Bust,' and the poem about the lady who throws her glove into the lions' den. Let those who say, 'Ah! but the poet must not defend what is contrary to right and decency,' remember heretic-burning and compulsory religion and be humble. Not perhaps right and wrong, but certainly our knowledge and groping understanding of them and their applications are in the highest degree mutable. Tennyson knew that:

> 'The hills are shadows, and they flow
> From form to form, and nothing stands.'

But neither he nor Milton—to instance two of our greatest didactic poets—realized that this was as true of our comprehension of ethics as of the facts of geography. Systems of ethics we must obviously have, for it is impossible for men to live in a community together without a pretty strict code. Civilized life is a tapestry woven of such codes. To take an apparently ridiculous instance, could twenty-two men amuse themselves for three days on a patch of green grass with two bats and a ball and six sticks if it were not for the M.C.C. rules of cricket? A system of ethics, enforced as rigidly as circumstances allow, is absolutely essential if men are to live together. It is difficult to over-estimate the harm done by a system of ethics which no longer fits the temper of the time, and whose decrees are consequently often broken, and these breaches visited now with severity, now with leniency. We are tempted to wish that some such device could be employed in morals as is used in certain minor questions of the code by which we live together; to long that the standard of morality to which the community expects us to conform were published every day in the newspaper like Lighting-up Time. Thus we should always know how to frame our own conduct in matters that affect our fellows and how we might expect our fellows to act in relation to us.

Perhaps so ridiculous an illustration will make the reader agree that this publication, this mere enunciation of what the community may from time to time agree shall be its working code of ethics, could clearly never be the prime work of the poet. Yet such is the sort of task which the didactics were inclined to believe was theirs.

The didactic poet, the poet who regards 'Art for Art's Sake' as the 'chiefest Lord of Hell,' has conceived his function to be that of helping to enforce the existing rules, and is apt to neglect his true function of devising, or of providing data for the devising of new and better rules. (Dr. Johnson, for instance, has a long passage in his preface to Shakespeare blaming him because he misses so many didactic opportunities.) That this was an unfortunate limitation of function the decorative artist saw. 'The chosen children of beauty,' the artists who conceived of their function as that of making human life endurable, of gladdening, if it might be, men's passage 'between a dark and a dark,' were uneasy at such a petrification.

But in repudiating the idea that the function of the poet was that of a judge, or, as they themselves would perhaps have said, of a kind of hortatory policeman, they went too far. They dissociated themselves completely from ethics. This weakened their position, and as consolers and makers of beauty they took rank below the makers of laws. For man is an intensely ethical animal; in the end ethics are among the three or four things he cares about most. And necessarily so, for ethics are the code by which he adapts himself to the extremely ticklish business of reconciling his inner biological needs with the circumstances of living in a community. The least mistake in this all-important sphere of the code and he feels that he may be seized and burnt at the stake or condemned to lifelong celibacy. So in dissociating themselves from all traffic with this absorbing affair the Decoratives cut themselves adrift from the main current of human life. Stevenson, a man of peculiarly clear vision, saw that such was the result of their creed, but he saw no way out of the decorative position except by joining with the Didactics whose tenets he could not accept. So he frankly said with a sigh that it must be acknowledged that the writer or the artist is but the *fille de joie* of the community. But the highest and the most serious function of the poet is to teach the law-makers—we are all in a smaller or greater degree law-makers—something about the human soul, sometimes to see beauty where before we had only seen shame and meanness, sometimes to tear the mask off pretension. This idea of the poet's function is not a new one. Certainly much of this simple doctrine of the poet or the prophet as the 'forth-teller,' though dark to Tennyson, was plain, for example, to the author of Ecclesiastes; he is as much concerned to give us a moving, sympathetic picture of the old man to whom the grasshopper is a burden and in whom desires have failed as he is to give us direct ethical instruction.

CHAPTER VIII

SYMBOLISM AND THE 'GHOST' THEORY

DIRECTLY we begin to deal with words, we begin to realise how shifting a thing is human language. The architect builds with square calculable stones, the musician with clear-cut, definite notes, but the poet has to use a stuff for his buildings which sometimes in a frenzy of despair he feels inclined to think will never stand still to be handled. A word is not only an extremely indefinite thing, but it is invariably also a composite thing. Look up any word in the dictionary, and you will find that it trails clouds of something or other behind it in its derivation from the Latin, Sanskrit, Greek, or Anglo-Saxon. You will probably find that the original word did not mean in the least what we mean by the word as we have it now, and we may find a whole string of meanings through which the word passed in the course of its handing down to us. Sometimes the derivations of a word give a sardonic comment upon human nature. It is always amusing, for instance, to think how typical it is of mankind's ways that 'presently' to Shakespeare and to Marlowe meant 'this moment.' But man is a procrastinating animal, and now the word openly means what it meant all along.

Ghosts of these former uses cling about words. Further, words pick up private family or class associations of their own on their way to us. We can all of us easily think of class Shibboleths. For example, there is nothing intrinsically shocking in the exchange of the phrases, 'Oh, beg pardon,' and 'Granted,' but in certain people the words will produce their shudder none the less, while to others they will appear completely harmless. Place names appear to be peculiarly sticky, I mean, to pick up associations particularly easily. The name of Vallombrosa, for instance, irresistibly calls up a train of its own, that is to anyone who is fond of 'Paradise Lost.' Perhaps a consideration of this train will illustrate the complexity of the associations with which words entangle themselves. To anyone with a visual imagination, the image called up by 'Vallombrosa' will probably first of all be a shallow stream with rounded boulders in it, and floating on it a glowing red-brown scum of leaves, each leaf curled up a little at the edge. Behind this image, there is another one, not so clear, and probably differing very markedly in the minds of different individual readers of Milton. This time it is a design, which might be in bas relief or might be in Chiaroscuro, of a landscape in which is a lake. The light is fitful, like that which we see just before a thunderstorm. Out of the lake half emerge figures in Roman armour—there are spears, helmets, bucklers, body armour, and short Roman swords, sometimes in the hands or on the persons of their wearers, sometimes piled along the side of the lake in great Baroque trophies. Somewhere in the middle of the lake reclines a gigantic shadowy figure, again in classical armour; a huge staff, 'fit for the mast of some high Amiral,' is the clearest of his attributes. A sense of despair and uneasiness hangs over the scene.

I do not mean that whenever the word 'Vallombrosa' is mentioned I stop and gaze for half an hour at these two super-imposed mental images. In reading a passage where the word occurred, I should be conscious of such pictures rather as one is conscious of decorations in a corridor down which one is passing. We see such pictures as we walk, the effect they produce may be sharp, but it is transitory. Their presence makes itself felt, however, and may colour our impressions of our other surroundings.

But the reader may ask: Why have you called such associations private? I have done so, because I suppose the mental image of a person who had visited Vallombrosa and had not read Milton would be completely different to mine, for instance, and this brings us to one of the points from which considerable complication springs. The association called up by a word may be, so to say, the association belonging to the word itself, or may belong to the thing expressed by the word. 'Municipal' may call up 'Mummy' from the position of the two words in the dictionary, or it might call up thoughts and images in connection with the word 'election,' or water supply, or tram system, or images allied with half a dozen other associations.

Some people again have a colour sense connected with words. Certain vowel and consonant sounds represent certain colours. To someone whom I know the sound of 'Ch' is red-brown, and the sound of 'S' represents yellow and gold. This fact emerged because this lady embroidered the names of my two daughters on a sash. Susan's embroidery was in yellow and gold, and Charlotte's in pinks, red and russets. She seemed surprised when I asked her why she had chosen these colours. The reason for using the silks seemed to her self-evident.

Miss Bryher, a young novelist who wrote a book called 'Development,' possesses something like the same sensory peculiarity. When such people read poetry, as far as I can make out, they experience, in addition to what the poet has set down for them, a sort of running accompaniment of colour patterns evoked not by the symbols employed by the poet—the green fields, the 'wine dark sea'—but by the sounds of the words employed.

We do not all re-act in quite such a complicated way, but to everybody each word necessarily becomes a kind of conglomeration or rather grows to be like an atom with its little court of electrons clustered round it. We are all, in writing prose or verse, in the case of our native language, consciously or unconsciously roughly aware of these associations that words carry with them, and we treat the words accordingly. Sometimes when we hear a foreigner talk, the fact that words do have very marked secondary characters of their own is brought home to us by the mistakes he will make through having apprehended only the obvious top meaning of a word. Nor is this all. Metaphysicians say that all knowledge is comparative, and our statements about things when analysed are found to consist in a placing of the thing spoken of into a category. Sometimes these categories are very exactly, sometimes very roughly conceived. We are confronted, say, by four material facts, a group of white daisies, a red geranium in a pot, a terrier asleep on the garden path, and a white pigeon pecking about for grains of corn amid the stones of the gravel. The most elaborate scientific classification of these creatures into vegetable and animal, bird and mammal, animate or inanimate, and so on through all the exactitudes of species, family and genus, are really only exact ways of saying that the geranium and the white daisies are more like each other than either is like the pigeon, or conversely that the dog and the pigeon are more alike than either is to the geranium or the pot. However far we push knowledge it never ceases to be relative.

This fact sometimes has curious consequences in the case of words. The most northerly county in Scotland, for instance, is called Sutherland, and, therefore, we can never speak or see its name without that word trailing after it some sort of image of the men who gave it that name, and of the country from which they came, and the black ships that brought them. Or, take the words 'kitten' or 'puppy,' which mean like a cat or like a dog, but less big and less mature. The words, because they are comparative, carry about with them a kind of back reference to cats and dogs. This is, of course, entirely obvious in words where a mere diminutive or superlative is formed—*super-man*, *duckling*. This reference to something on one side or the other of the actual thing meant by the word is another of the electrons clustering round the word-atom.

But we have a third trick of the human brain to reckon with, and that is our primitive habit of personifying. At one time or another, man seems to have personified everything under the sun—the seasons, his own emotions, the sea, colds in the head, all the different aspects of the forces that play upon him (destinies, furies, devils, mystery gods, and so forth). This personification or symbolism was in fact probably the only process by which primitive minds were able to deal with abstract thought at all. Personification, though it seems natural and easy enough to us even now (that is, if we are careful not to stop to consider the mental processes that it involves), in primitive society was probably a process which seized upon any more or less abstract idea which happened to enter a man's mind,—just in the same way that the process of digestion seized upon any article of food that entered his body.

Such then are words. Here is the sort of stuff which writers have to use. But the electrons do not have the same value in poetry and prose alike. In the case of prose, the reader is to a certain extent hurried on by the sense of the passage that he is reading past the comparative implications which the word may carry with it, past the symbolic meaning. In prose the word is much more a vehicle than it is in poetry. Nothing is commoner than for a quick reader in the case of prose to read a passage and to take in the sense of it clearly, but not to be able to recollect one phrase or word in which that meaning was conveyed to him. It is hardly to be supposed that anyone has ever read poetry like that. In the case of a quick, inattentive reader, it is more likely to be the other way about. He may know the colour and flavour of the poem, but not necessarily be very clear what its subject was.

It comes about, therefore, that the prose writer's task, so far as purely verbal expression is concerned, is the easier one. Half these elusive, shifting, secondary meanings, implications and associations are in his case, slurred over and almost ignored. Thus he makes his patterns with more or less straightforward material, and has done with it. But the poet is always making a pattern in two or three dimensions at once, and the clash in the sub-pattern made by the under-tones, under-meanings, under-associations of his words and phrases may, by some effect of bathos, or through some other cause, completely ruin his apparently excellent and sensible top meaning. And this having to consider four or five things at once, of course makes his task difficult. There is, however, obviously a credit side to this account. One may, in fact, to some extent liken a poem to a kaleidoscope picture, most of whose grand effect is made not by the little bits of glass which the shake of our hand has arranged, but from the reflections of these pieces of glass in the mirrors which form its sides. So in a great number of poems it is the symbolism and under-tones and implications when combined and contrasted with its obvious straightforward meaning that give the piece of verse all its richness. Too great a reliance upon the symbolic and 'ghost' sides of poetry is, however, as we should expect, not without its pitfalls. Psychologists seem to think that there does exist a small group of words to which all people, using the same language, attach the same symbolic meaning, but the number of such words is small, and may grow smaller as varied reading replaces original images with acquired ones. Consequently it sometimes happens that a word to the poet may bring up a perfectly different train of ghosts to the one which it brings up to the reader (as in the case of 'Vallombrosa'). The result is, of course, if his top meaning is negligible, that the poet talks in a kind of private cypher of his own. The most obvious case of this is Blake's Books of Prophecy. There do apparently (or least there might) exist people to whom the mystical meaning of what Blake wrote is as clear as it was to Blake, but to most people the key to Blake's thought is lost, because his meaning was expressed exclusively in the shifting, ghostly, shadowy mediums of association and symbolism.

The consideration of this side of poetry is further complicated by the fact that symbol 'allegory,' 'metaphor,' 'simile,' and 'comparison,' all seem to be words which in practice are used as if they shaded into one another. The distinction between them is far from clear in my own mind, but the situation seems to me roughly to be that all these things are methods of indirect statement. We might perhaps define a symbol as a statement by indirect means which the reader does not mentally translate back into 'plain English.' In the case of allegory, on the other hand, most of the effect is produced by the fact that he does. When we go to see 'Everyman' acted, a great deal of our pleasure appears to me to spring from the fact that we are continuously engaged in a mental process of translating back 'Mankind,' 'Sin,' 'Good Deeds,' and 'Death' into little concrete statements. 'Good Deeds' is a piece of religious allegory. We translate it back. The Christian symbols of the Lamb or the Cross, the Pagan symbols of Proserpine and Balder, the Universal symbol of the woman with the infant on her knee, wo do not translate back. Is it perhaps possible that a symbol is an allegory so well known, so firmly accepted, and hence so obvious that we can think in its terms as easily as in any other? Metaphor, simile, and analogy seem to me to be methods of expression rather than methods of thought. Such devices are most frequently used to reduce the general to the particular, the abstract to the concrete. They are ways of making the general easier of apprehension to the minds of the reader or the listener. Only those who have habitually to employ them know what untrustworthy servants they sometimes prove.

In Professor Whitehead's opinion words are invariably slightly misleading. He, considering language from the point of view of the mathematician, is, in fact, so appalled by the amount of back meanings, associations, and generally by the 'ghosts' which we have tried to show in this chapter that he rejects words altogether as not being fit for the expression of exact ideas at all. I cite Professor Whitehead because I do not want the reader to suppose that all this business is a sort of feverish dream, a figment of the brain of neurotic poets, and that language is really pretty exact and four square after all. It was his complete conviction of the unstableness and above all of the 'vital' character of words that induced Professor Whitehead to evolve his system of symbolic logic. He was in a region where figures would not altogether serve his turn, but rather than use such myriad-faceted, ungovernable things as words in the statement of nice and exact shades of logical meaning, he substitutes dots, dashes, pluses, and equals—any material, however humble, that he can trust to stand still to be manipulated. But Professor Whitehead is not the only scientist to react from the tyranny of words. There is a whole School of Science—Mr.

Sanderson of Oundle is the spokesman through whom it was expounded to me—who, whenever possible, substitute charts, graphs, and tables for the written word.

Of this school of thought I shall speak in a later chapter.

Chapter IX

USES AND ABUSES OF METRE

As far as our intellects are concerned, the pleasure we take in Metre has, I fancy, to do with our pleasure in the familiar. The difference between prose and metre has been stated graphically as the difference between a line which is constantly curving back upon itself and a line which goes forward all the time. The whole point of most of the devices of metre is the recurrence of particular thoughts or rhythms either exactly, or with a small change. The rhyme itself is, of course, a perfect example of this. What the reader enjoys is the return to a similar sound, and a different sense.

But really the main function of metre is the hypnotic one which I tried to analyse three chapters ago. But why should the well-marked repetitions of the dance, the recurrence of a refrain, or the more subtle backward curving of rhyme and antithesis have this lulling and soothing effect upon us, quite apart from any symbolism in the dance, or any meaning in the words? Is it possible that these rhythms make some subtle union with the natural rhythms of our bodies? For the life of the body is full of rhythms—there are the alternations of sleeping and waking, the ebb and flow of our breathing, the intricate heart pattern of systole and diastole, the motion of our legs in walking, the dozen internal rhythms of contraction and relaxation of which we are not conscious, and lastly that curious rhythmic agony of the birth pangs which have brought each of us into the world. The human race seems to have a natural passion for recurrence and rhythmic curves, and is always looking out for them. Our clocks and watches really go along straightforward *tick-tick-tick*, but most of use to please our rhythm-hunger, hear the sounds as *tick-tock*. There are dozens of everyday sounds that we conventionalise and regularise for our pleasure, the sound of the wheels of trains and trams, the ripplings and murmur of brooks and rivers, the beat of waves. Without rhythm and its effect upon the subconsciousness, and its power of direct non-intellectual command over the body, most drill and all concerted music and dancing would be impossible. The unaided will could never time a muscular contraction within half a breath as will a rhythmic cycle:

> 'Let your feet
> Like the galleys when they row
> Even beat.'

But to return to the actual problems set us by our use of these rhythmic powers in poetry. There are, of course, a whole set of arguments for and against regularity of poetic metre. Let us first consider the objections to the use of strict forms. In the first place, from being capable servants, rhyme and metre may obviously become the most tyrannical masters, entirely intractable to the poet's will, the implacable enemies of the *mot juste.* Especially is metre apt to become the enemy of thought:

> 'For rhymes the rudders are of verses
> By which like ships they steer their courses.'

If he embarks on too elaborate a metrical scheme, the poet will often find himself unable to call his soul his own. All this business of prosody and metre also has been complicated by the frantic attempts of scholars to fit Latin forms of prosody and scansion on to English. As far as I can understand this most complicated controversy, what has been proved is that they very nearly fit, but not quite. The Prosodists are much in the position of somebody who tries to put the left boot on to the right foot. He justly pleads that the boot is of the right size, that it is the right sort of boot, and that surely it ought to fit and can be made to do so. Even to this day a great many scholars and experts have not discovered what is wrong.

Many a young person has been for ever frightened off any consideration of poetry by his complete inability to understand the difference—except in the isolation of 'examples'—between iambs, trochees, anapaests, and dactyls. I remember quite well how when I was about sixteen, I struggled with this very business, and how a kind mentor wrote me out syllables in longs and shorts, and how I faithfully pinned them over my washstand and conned them until I knew them. Then I tried to fit them on to the poetry I knew by heart; I never dared confess that it seemed to me possible to scan most of it at least in two ways. I tore my hair and then and there grimly decided that poetry was not for me, as I apparently could not understand, or, at any rate, could not apply what appeared to be universally acknowledged as the very foundation of poetic technique. It was not till years afterwards that I discovered that the great majority of English poems can in sober fact be scanned in two or three ways, and that there is much to be said for the theory that the whole of this elaborate science of prosody is just(but how completely!) beside the point in the case of English verse. If only it had occurred to somebody to reveal the simple fact to me that almost all beginners write first by ear and then 'dress' their syllables by the primitive method of counting them up on their fingers, and that this habit was no unique shame of mine! Also that not till I came to the stage of this counting-on-fingers process would I necessarily be sure where the beginning of the lines and the capital letters came. However, enough of my youthful sorrows. I am quite ready to agree with the reader that if my poetic impulse was stifled by this sort of mechanical difficulty it was not of very strong growth and not particularly well worth preserving.

A study of formal Prosody seems to breed very much the same temper in its students as do acrostics or jig-saw puzzles. We mark the same glittering eye, the same absorption, the same enthusiasm. But I do beg the enthusiasts to remember that their pastime is a game, and not to confuse it with the study of poetry.

The following passage will serve to remind the reader of the immense volume of literature of which it is typical. When written in America, this sort of analysis is apt to go one further in abstraction and to take the form of some sort of chart or graph. This particular passage was written by a man with a real power of appreciating poetry. Its subject is Tennyson's *Tithonus*:

> 'As in *Ulysses,* the movement is slow and regular; but it is varied in a different manner. Inversions are fewer; there are but 7 beginning inversions, an average of 9 per cent., and there is 1 caesural inversion. Weak measures are slightly more abundant, 48 per cent., and the failure of the stress in the fourth measure amounts to a characteristic of the rhythm. One-half of the weak measures, 18, fall in this place; there are 9 in the third position, 4 in the fifth, and 3 and 2 in the first and second, respectively. There are 21 spondees or 28 per cent., and the frequency of these in the second measure constitutes another characteristic of the rhythm. The second position, with 9, is followed by the first with 6; the third has 4, and the fourth and fifth, 1 each. There is less than average frequency of run-on, 26 per cent. But one of the most striking characteristics of the rhythm is the extraordinary number of lines without interior pause, 35, or 46 per cent. So that while the proportion of end-stops is usually great there is still an unusually high exponent of fluency, 3.37.'

It was chiefly in its capacity as the enemy of the *mot juste* that the Imagists fell foul of regular metre and endeavoured to set up in its stead their cadenced verses, but it is amusing to see the way in which their cadences immediately became almost as tyrannical as a strict form like the sonnet. We have rather a good instance of this in Miss Amy Lowell's *Patterns*:—

> 'I walk down the garden paths,
> And all the daffodils
> Are blowing, and the bright blue squills.
> I walk down the patterned garden paths
> In my stiff brocaded gown.
> With my powdered hair and jewelled fan,
> I too am a rare
> Pattern. As I wander down
> The garden paths.
>
> 'My dress is richly figured,
> And the train
> Makes a pink and silver stain
> On the gravel, and the thrift
> Of the borders.
> Just a plate of current fashion,
> Tripping by in high-heeled, ribboned shoes.
> Not a softness anywhere about me,
> Only whalebone and brocade.
> And I sink on a seat in the shade
> Of a lime tree. For my passion
> Wars against the stiff brocade.
> The daffodils and squills
> Flutter in the breeze
> As they please.
> And I weep;
> For the lime tree is in blossom
> And one small flower has dropped upon my bosom.'

This is the opening of the poem and the threads are caught up and repeated at the end. Mrs. Wilkinson gives an interesting analysis of it in her book *New Voices* :—

> 'This poem is designed in cadences, and in spite of its great variety, the symmetry is to be found, first of all, in the repetition, at more or less regular intervals, of the typical or pattern cadence of the poem, "In my stiff brocaded gown." (It is the cadence that is repeated, not the words.) The cadence is reiterated in lines like the following :—
>
> "Makes a pink and silver stain"
> "Only whalebone and brocade"
> "Underneath my stiffened gown"
> "But she guesses he is near"
> "With the weight of this brocade"
> "By each button, hook and lace"
> "Aching, melting, unafraid."
>
> 'In other lines we find this cadence varies just a little bit. Perhaps an accent will be changed, perhaps a word with two short-sounding syllables will be substituted for a word with one long-sounding syllable, thus giving the line a new effect with the same time value as the typical cadence. (For there is certainly such a thing as quantity in English poetry, and the greatest poets have felt it and used their knowledge of it, although they have not argued about it overmuch.) Such slightly varied lines are like the following :—
>
> "Just a plate of current fashion"
> And the sliding of the water'
> Bewildered by my laughter
> Underneath the fallen blossoms
> Fighting with the Duke in Flanders."'

Is not the tyranny of the cadence apparent? No poet not bitterly constrained by his form, would write such a line as :—

> 'Just a plate of current fashion . . .'

or use that shocking word 'tripping.' The phraseology of the whole poem is an outrage! But we do not feel all the indignation with Miss Lowell that we might feel, because we realise that she is not really writing poetry at all, but making a metrical experiment. But such technique is a curious result of all the protestations of the *vers librists*!

Mr. Maurice Baring is a poet who has written very elaborately-constructed *vers libre*. His beautiful rhymed poem 'In Memoriam' to Lord Lucas is a good example of the technique of this form. The poem is very carefully tied together. He often uses verbal repetition to fulfil the function of regular metre, for example:—

> 'I brushed the dream away, and quite forgot
> The nightmare's ugly blot.
> So was the dream forgot. The dream came true.'

Here is the Hebrew device, only both sense and words are repeated, not sense alone, as in 'A man of sorrow and acquainted with grief,' which represents the usual Hebrew form. But the best passage in the poem comes with the climax of the narrative:—

> 'And after days of watching, days of lead,
> There came the certain news that you were dead.
> You had died fighting, fighting against odds,
> Such as in war the gods
> Aethereal dared when all the world was young;
> Such fighting as blind Homer never sung,
> Nor Hector nor Achilles never knew;
> High in the empty blue.
>
> High, high, above the clouds, against the setting sun,
> The fight was fought, and your great task was done.'

There is one inconvenience which haunts all

irregular metre, and that is that, no normal having been established, the reader does not always know how the poet wants his quantities and emphasis arranged. For in a regular poem the general beat of the lines serve as implied stage directions to the reader in any doubtful passage. If in *vers libre* the quantities are understood wrongly the result may be the accidental changing round of accented and unaccented parts of the line, and this may make a considerable difference even in the sense, But, of course, the whole question of free or strict metre is one of balance. There are certain great obvious advantages in the use of rhyme and of strict metre. Besides its wonderful power of clinching and emphasising a statement rhyme is delightful in itself. Frankau's ' One of Us ' or Byron's ' Don Juan ' would be stripped as bare by the omission of female rhymes as by the omission of female characters.

This business of rhyme and metre has, of course, also got to be considered in conjunction with poetic architecture. The proper choice of the pattern of the poem will obviously be affected by the scale. A villanelle is charming, but imagine a long narrative poem in a succession of them? When we consider this balance, this choice between the exact thought and beautiful word and the regularity of metre, let us never forget one thing—that is, not to sell our souls to the devil and then not get the price. Which brings us back again to the consideration of prosody. There are certain principles concerning the reader which the writer must never forget. Many rhyme schemes have been worked out by prosodists, many arrangements of cæsuras, pauses, of emphatic and unemphatic syllables which the reader will never in this world detect. Most readers cannot, for instance, carry a rhyme in their heads for more than four lines, and there are a thousand and one systems of chain rhymes, hidden alliterations, and so on, which can be at the same time extremely crippling to the poet's sense, and null and void to the reader. Of course there exist many poems which are valuable and beautiful solely on account of their rhythms and of their actual physical sound arrangements, poems in which sense and niceness of vocabulary are both secondary. Such poems have been written at all dates, and they are common to all countries—Persian literature is full of them, the Elizabethans constantly wrote them, Tennyson delighted in them. Such poems are not much written nowadays though search would reveal instances of this pure 'singing' in Mr. Graves' and Mr. de la Mare's work, and I think the following three verses from a war poem by Mr. Brett Young (a poet, alas! now turned novelist) will justify the labour that we may choose to give to the study of rhythm :—

> 'Through Porton village, under the bridge
> A clear bourne floweth, with grasses trailing,
> Wherein are shadows of white clouds sailing,
> And elms that shelter under the ridge.
>
> 'Over the bridge where the shallow races,
> Under a clear and frosty sky;
> And the winterbourne, as we marched by.
> Mirrored a thousand laughing faces.

'By stagnant waters we lie rotten.
On windless nights, in the lonely places,
There, where the winter water races,
O, Porton river, are we forgotten?'

The images are not particularly good, in fact we are not very much convinced that the marching battalion could be reflected in 'racing shallows.' The sky seems to be both cloudy and clear at the same time, whilst the contrast between the English and the Flemish countryside has been made many times. Again 'floweth' is a disagreeable archaism, and so is 'wherein.' But how obviously silly and beside the point are such criticisms! The poet has not been aiming at perfection along these lines; he has been trying to make a lovely piece of music, and he has made it. The reader will probably find the tune and rhythm running in his head apart from the words.

II

There is one last minor point that I should like to consider here, and that is the relations of voice and verse, of musical and poetic rhythms. I propose to consider it exclusively from the poet's point of view because ignorance of music makes me apprehend their combination from this standpoint naturally, and also because it is a point of view which has been too little considered. I think that all critics, literary and musical, are of opinion that there is something wrong with such a setting as say 'Rule Britannia': —

'The na-tions no-o-o-o-ot so blessed a-a-as thou
Shall i-i-i-i-i-i-i-in their turn to ty-y-y-y-rants fall.'

Some modern poets are of opinion that music is always more or less inimical to poetry when it is coupled with it. They would have us say our lyrics and sing 'Do, Ray, Me,' or in an uncomprehended foreign language which is the same thing. On the other hand, the Hammersmith production of *The Beggar's Opera* undoubtedly shows us examples of music and words which are insignificant apart, but which joined together form a whole that is irresistible. When we come to print it, there is really nothing in such a song as this without its melting air :—

> 'If the heart of a man is oppressed with cares,
> The mist is dispelled if a woman appears;
> Like the notes of a fiddle, she sweetly, sweetly
> Raises our spirits and charms our ears.'

But musicians say that there is very little in the melting air without the seductive words. Together they are, as the young lady in Fielding would say, 'pure.'

That is why I don't think that I can quite agree with Mr. Vachel Lindsay, who does not consider that words and music can ever make a whole satisfactory to a person who cares for poetry. But to consider some modern songs. Lord Berner's setting, for instance, of a pleasing, undistinguished 'Lullaby' of Dekker's makes too much of the words. He kills them with over-emphasis.

Mr. Eugene Goosens has tried to be onomatopoeic with Richard Barnefield's 'Philomel'; the beginning of it alone is effective :

> 'As it fell upon a day
> In the merry month of May,

Sitting in a pleasant shade
Which a grove of myrtles made,
Beasts did leap and birds did sing,
Trees did grow and plants did spring.'

So far, so good—a delightful tripping tune.

'Everything did banish moan
Save the nightingale alone:
She, poor bird, as all forlorn,
Lean'd her breast up till a thorn
And there sung the dolefull'st ditty,
That to hear it was great pity.'

All this woe Mr. Goossens took far too seriously, and later on when the poet mourns with her:—

'Ah! thought I, thou mourn'st in vain,
None take pity on thy pain:
Senseless trees, they cannot hear thee,
Ruthless beasts they will not cheer thee;
King Pandion he is dead,
All thy friends are lapp'd in lead';

he takes the affair almost *au grand tragique*. The fact is, of course, that the rhythmical changes of the verse itself are quite emphasis enough for the mild academic passion of the poem. Sir Thomas Wyatt's 'Appeal' has real passion, and of this Mr. Eugene Goossens in his setting has made full use. Was it not also partly successfully wedded to the music because, like the lyrics in *The Beggar's Opera*, it has a rather unsatisfactory flat rhythm of its own?:

'And wilt thou leave me thus,
That hath given thee my heart
Never for to depart,
Neither for pain nor smart:
And wilt thou leave me thus?
Say nay! Say nay!'

Miss Frances Cornford's delicate 'The Ragwort' is largely swamped by Mr. Arthur Bliss's music, but 'The Dandelion' (by the same author and set by the same composer) is an admirable example of a happy alliance between voice and verse:—

'The children with their simple hearts,
The lazy men that ride in carts,
The little dogs that lollop by,
They all have seen its shining eye;
And every one of them would say
They never saw a thing so gay.'

Here again the rhythm is not intrinsically strong, and therefore the poem proves ductile to the music. Mr. Bliss has even been bold enough to introduce repetition into the words: this, instead of being disagreeable, proves delightful. 'The Dandelion,' of which I have quoted the second verse, is a very tightly packed short poem, and we are glad to have '*simple hearts, simple hearts,*' and 'little dogs that lollop by, *lollop by, lollop by.*' One would say at a venture that Mr. Bliss was fond of poetry, for even in this very well finished little poem there are weak places, and he does not, with the usual fiendish pleasure of musicians, pounce upon these, dwell upon them, and draw them out until the unfortunate listener squirms with the verbal infelicities. No, he covers them up almost as would an intelligent reader.

Chapter X

POETIC ARCHITECTURE

Perhaps the thing that has been most often remarked about modern poetry is the fact that, except by Mr. Masefield, very few long poems have been written. There has been some discussion as to the cause of this, those who do not like modern poetry of course saying that it is because the present age lacks the strength for sustained inspiration. Perhaps a study of some of those long poems of the past which have not been wholly successful will give us the best notion of why the modern poet, for the most part, writes short poems.

Every poet, as Mr. Sturge Moore has observed, when he comes by a bit of the true gold, has to piece his treasure out with a greater or less proportion of 'any material that comes handy' before he can make a poem out of it, because we do not demand that a poet should be a jeweller. We want an architect or sculptor. But there is something in the very nature of poetic inspiration which makes it improbable that, unaided by a more pedestrian faculty, it should be capable of producing a whole at all. Shelley in his 'Defence of Poetry' gives a very good account of the 'afflatus' and its necessary succession by a secondary faculty:—

> 'The mind in creation is as a fading coal, which some invisible influence, like an inconstant wind, awakens to transitory brightness; this power arises from within, like the colour of a flower which fades and changes as it is developed, and the conscious portions of our nature are unprophetic either of its approach or its departure. Could this influence be durable in its original purity and force, it is impossible to predict the greatness of the results; but when composition begins, inspiration is already on the decline, and the most glorious poetry that has ever been communicated to the world is probably a feeble shadow of the original conceptions of the poet . . .
>
> 'The toil and the delay recommended by critics, can be justly interpreted to mean no more than a careful observation of the inspired moments, and an artificial connection of the spaces between their suggestions, by the intertexture of conventional expressions; a necessity only imposed by the limitedness of the poetical faculty itself.'

The modern poet must still add his bits here and there, and piece out the results of his first poetic impulse with his 'intertexture of conventional expressions.' But whereas Wordsworth, often almost, so to say, buried his gold idol under its feet of clay, the modern poet, even where his gold is rather scanty, adds as little as possible, and—when his poem is a failure—often produces an idol not only with no feet at all, but without anything whatever to stand upon. On the whole, however, the impulse—a horror-struck flying from the long and the tiresome—is a good one. It certainly enables a poet to speak to a larger audience. The vast tomes of what we may call secondary material produced by some of our greatest poets, form a serious barrier to many readers. It is often a barrier which the most careful anthologizing cannot surmount, for the gold and the clay may be absolutely inextricable. On the other hand, of course, the modern poet's self-denying ordinance cuts him off not only from certain aesthetic effects but from a certain sort of reader who desires narrative. It is probably as much because he writes narrative poems as because on the whole he remains the best modern poet that Mr. Masefield is the most widely-read of his contemporaries.

What are these aesthetic effects which can only be achieved by means of a long poem? The reader will remember the climax of 'The Everlasting Mercy' when the hero walks out on a fresh February morning and watches the man ploughing, hears the birds and sees the sunrise and the first light glittering on the cobwebs, and turns and praises God. Detached from its context, this is a beautiful passage, but its effect is incomparably heightened by its being used as the climax to the realism and often brutality of the earlier part of the narrative.

Another effect of the mere length of a poem is that the reader gets into the mood of it. The poet dare attempt to be more strange or subtle in his atmosphere in a long poem. This effect becomes pretty obvious if we try reading such a poem as 'Endymion' through and then dipping into it and taking selected passages. In reading solidly through it we cannot help being caught in the glamour of that whole magic world, our mood is a pale shadow of Keats' when he wrote it. In this life of enchantment the weaknesses of the poem are forgotten: our spirit is melted by its soft beauties: we no longer want to blame, hardly to criticise, hardly to think which are the passages of greatest merit. But open the poem here and there and you will find yourself turning on to some of the more splendid passages—the description of Adonis' bower, where a Cupid kneels playing a harp, 'Muting to death the pathos with his wings,' or the description of Circe and the 'haggard scene' when she taunts and torments her train of beasts and the poor elephant pleads vainly for release from the gross flesh in which she has imprisoned him.

Take again another kind of atmosphere, the effects that Mr. Masefield gets in 'Dauber'—the fatigue and weariness of the terrible weeks off Cape Horn, the pitiless iteration of the storm, the wretchedness, exhaustion, and peril. All this could not possibly have been brought before us in a few lines. The work is done cumulatively, the effects are elaborately led up to, our minds are prepared for the restless desolation, the strain and agony of this prolonged physical wretchedness.

If Chinese or Japanese conciseness could not possibly give us these effects, obviously on the other hand certain notions gain tremendously by shortness and simplicity of statement. Take the following—one of Mr. Waley's incomparable 'Translations from the Chinese.' The effects which the poet,

Po Chü-I, is aiming at here, appear to me to be, first, that which painters often try to get in rendering an interior, a feeling of being shut in, of enclosure, of intimacy. With this is connected the psychological introvertion caused by illness; the sick man by reason of the illness is necessarily concerned with his own body, and this inevitably leads him to the consideration of his own mind. Then this notion of physical and spiritual 'shut-in-ness' is to be shown giving way to a larger vision, but the reader is to keep the tranquillity of the Quietist with his consciousness that 'The world is too much with us.'

Sick Leave.

'Propped on pillows, not attending to business;
For two days I've lain behind locked doors.
I begin to think that those who hold office
Get no rest, except by falling ill!
For restful thoughts one does not need space;
The room where I lie is ten foot square.
By the western eaves, above the bamboo twigs,
From my couch I see the White Mountain rise,
But the clouds that hover on its far-distant peak
Bring shame to a face that is buried in the World's dust.'

The shortness of the poem exactly suits the nature of the ideas which the poet intends to convey. An extra line or two, further descriptions of sensations, room, or landscape, would have weakened the sharpness of the impression.

Japanese poems are shorter still. The 'tanka,' of five lines, is the form in which almost all Japanese poetry is written, and for centuries the poetic inspiration of this language has been confined to a plot of ground far narrower than that of the sonnet. There are many poems in Japanese consisting of three lines only. Here are three examples, again from Mr. Waley's translations :—

FUJIWARI NO OKIKAZE.

'With voice unceasing
Sing, O nightingale!
In one year
Even as much as twice
Can Spring come?'

HITOMARO (?).

'My thoughts are with a boat
Which travels island-hid
In the morning mist
Off the shore of Akashi—
Dim, dim!'

ANON.

'O cuckoo,
Because the villages where you sing
Are so many,
I am estranged from you, even
In the midst of my love!'

This last poem the commentator says 'He speaks in a parable to a girl that had many hearts.' This explanation brings us to the consideration of some of the qualities which shortness will make us value in a poem. Only in a short poem could the anonymous writer's little frail 'touch and go" allegory have been stated just so, and only by an audience who realised the *double èntendre* that is intended can the five lines be properly enjoyed. It is nearly always a small, close, highly-civilised literary society that produces such poems. Such a poem is really the half word addressed to the right hearer. It relies upon allusion, upon the double meaning which must not be pressed too far.

Japanese and Chinese poetry and the poems of the Greek anthology have all of them something of the quality of attar of roses; the poet's thought and intention has been distilled down. The tiny size of the poem makes us conscious of an immense work of selection and self-denial—the poet had a great deal to say, but not choosing to leave his reader with a blurred image, chose only this, the very essential oil of his thought. But being poetry, and therefore unlike a direct statement in 'two words,' this potent drop spreads by implication its aroma—bitter or sweet—over a wide tract.

II

LET us consider the case of the poet who, desiring to produce a given effect, express a given thought, sits down to consider whether it shall be expressed in an epic or an epigram. In all probability, of course, no poet has ever done such a thing, for, as Shelley says somewhere, 'every artist worth the name is something of an artificer'; inspiration and a general sense of its proper technical expression should be simultaneous births. But if a poet ever did find himself in this impossible situation of knowing very well what he wanted to say, but having no idea of how to say it, he would, as far as length is concerned, find himself pulled by two different impulses. Earlier in the book, in trying to define poetry, I said I believed that we should find that one of its essential characteristics is compression, and gave as an example Keats' 'Ode to a Nightingale,' together with a most unsuccessful prose rendering of two verses of it, which expressed half as many ideas in twice as many words. The poet would find then on the one hand that the fact that he intended to express his thoughts in verse would tend to shorten them, they would automatically, to borrow a metaphor from the kitchen, 'reduce' and 'thicken.' On the other hand, in writing poetry ideas have a tendency to shoot like a twig in the spring. 'Lo fresh Flora has flourished every spray!' The dry stick of a concept is apt to double its size by putting forth leaves and flowers, often flowers of illustration. We can see these two processes at work very clearly in the case of eighteenth century writers—indeed, the period has an inestimable dissecting-room value—Poets were then often quite consciously engaged in the pursuit of writing alternate epigrams, *i.e.* a couplet or, at most, two couplets of intensely reduced matter—and then throwing out a sort of bow window of a metaphor beginning probably 'Thus when' or 'As thus.' Young will afford the diligent reader capital examples of what I mean. He would write such lines as:—

> 'Autumnal Lycie carries in her face
> Memento mori to each public place';

and then next moment would let an idea shoot and blossom out from a 'So have we seen' like so much

Bindweed, until it half covered the garden plot of his page.

This question of length is very often one upon which young writers stumble. Till he becomes a true craftsman, when inspiration and the technique which expresses it will rise entwined into his consciousness, we shall often find the young poet expressing a pleasing, simple concept in a diluted rambling form and producing a bad poem; sometimes all such a poem wants is to be boiled down and made into an essence. Many a piece of metred prose could be restored to a state of poetry by a mere process of condensation. Again we sometimes see—these cases are rarer—inexpert poets whose thoughts are subtle, but who feel their energies flagging over sustained work, and who therefore—(unwilling to sacrifice their subtlety)—produce short poems either of incomprehensible crabbedness or poems which are, so to speak, hollow. The reader is conscious that the poet is trying to give him something, but the thought has escaped from the cage in which he tried to put it. The reader has a sensation which he may very very likely express by saying that there is 'nothing in' the poem. This is a trouble which is specially apt to occur in a case where the poet has tried to use symbolic phraseology.

Chapter XI

POETIC SUGGESTION

A work of art, may, besides being considered as a thing in itself, be regarded as an instrument with which to affect the minds of others. If my theory that poetry is primarily a subtle, communicating medium is a correct one, a careful consideration of what we may call the 'receiving end' of the poem is obviously worth while. But thought for the reader is just what poets are occasionally apt, with a *beau geste* to refuse to take, at any rate, consciously. When I say poets in this instance, I really mean English poets, for the poets of the classical tradition, the tradition of the greater part of French, Spanish, and Italian prose and verse, have always kept this side of their business well in mind. Flaubert, in writing of the novel enlarges on the point. As long as he is reading, the reader's emotions are to be controlled, his mind is to be canalised. His powers are to be directed in a certain way, the pace of his reading is to be regulated, he is to become the creature—the puppet—of the artist to whose suggestion he, in the act of reading, submits himself.

The reader should just as much become the servant of the poet, a fact which was perceived by

Dryden when he wrote *Alexander's Feast.* Here Timotheus

> '. . . placed on high,
> Amid the tuneful quire,'

seems to regard the resources of his art rather as a doctor might regard the British Pharmacopoeia. Here is a drug, a strain of the lyre, by means of which he can quicken the patient's pulse, here another by which he can retard it. Here is a stimulant by which he can rouse him to energy. Here is a depressant (a sort of poetical salycilate) by which he can plunge him into the depths of pessimism. Here is opium which can make the victim slough off in a drowsy ecstacy all care for this world and the next. Here is an aphrodisaic by which he can make him believe 'the world well lost for love.'

So Timotheus—apparently by means of classical allusions in whose efficacy we do not quite believe—first brings Alexander to believe himself a second Jove.

> 'With ravish'd ears
> The monarch hears,
> Assumes the god,
> Affects to nod,
> And seems to shake the spheres.'

Next Timotheus sings of Bacchus, the beautiful, the light of heart, in triumphant jollity:—

> 'Bacchus, ever fair and young,
> Drinking joys did first ordain;
> Bacchus' blessings are a treasure,
> Drinking is the soldier's pleasure:
> Rich the treasure,
> Sweet the pleasure;
> Sweet is pleasure after pain.'

'Soothed with the sound, the king grew vain;
Fought all his battles o'er again;
And thrice he routed all his foes, and thrice he slew the slain.'

But the King grew tiresome in his synthetic cups, and Timotheus, choosing a mournful muse, switches him off and sings of poor Darius, who, though great and good, was 'overcome by fate':—

'Fallen, fallen, fallen, fallen,
Fallen from his high estate,
And weltering in his blood.'

Alexander's mood again responds, and he grows 'the joyless victor,' and sighs in pity at the blind turns of chance. Timotheus smiles to see his charm work, and holding that love is next to pity,

'Softly sweet, in Lydian measures,
Soon he soothed his soul to pleasures.
War, he sung, is toil and trouble;
Honour, but an empty bubble;
Never ending, still beginning,
Fighting still, and still destroying;
"If the world be worth the winning,
Think, O think it worth enjoying!
Lovely Thais sits beside thee,
Take the good the gods provide thee!"
The many rend the skies with loud applause;
So love was crown'd, but music won the cause.'

After this, however, Alexander apparently got thoroughly drunk, and in the rest of his vicissitudes, Timotheus was unfairly assisted by Bacchus.

Of course, the modern poet is met at once with a difficulty, unknown to the old experimenter. Timotheus had his Alexander before him, and could watch the effects of his enchantment, or, to resume the medical metaphor, could be sure that his patient was taking his medicine regularly, and reacting normally. It is in the matter of this closeness of relation between poet and audience that the coterie is so useful. A coterie is really formed by any company of people who have read the same books and seen the same plays, and among whom are to be found auditors and performers. If the poet believes himself to be appealing chiefly to a particular circle, whose antecedents and tastes he to some extent understands, he is able in his poetry to use many means which are, in the case of audiences who are an unknown quantity, impossible to him. As I said in the chapter on Poetic Architecture, Greek, Japanese, and Chinese lyric poetry are cases in point. Most of such poems are very brief—the Japanese tanka is only five lines long—and the poet produces a great part of his effects by allusion. Now allusion is one of the most useful of poetic devices; it is to be classed as an overt sort of symbolism. If you say the four names 'King Lear, Jehu, Robinson Crusoe, Mr. Greatheart,' to me, and if you know that I have been brought up in England, you can calculate that such and such images will be called up in my mind.

We may not know each other personally, but from the fact that you are pretty sure that I have read that which will enable me to take your meaning, you and I are in a comparatively good position to communicate with one another. If you knew nothing about me at all except the fact that I was able to read English, in trying to affect my emotions, you would be very much in the position of a doctor who had to prescribe for a patient he had never seen. You would only be able to use a very limited range of drugs, drugs to which all human beings were known to respond.

Now it might be that it would do just as well in your poem if you said that a lady was more chaste than Dorigen, or more voluptuous than Aquilina, that a philosopher was more sophistical than Dr. Pangloss, an architect another Halvard Solness, but you could not be sure that I as 'the general reader,' should know what you meant and, therefore, these excellent comparisons would be useless as a means of conveying your meaning to me except possibly as pleasantly bemusing scraps of rhetoric.

If then you are ambitious, and are not content to write for a minority of known cultivation, if you aspire to an almost universal comprehension, you will have in the case of all your secondary material to go rather far back and consider what are the images, allusions, metaphors and associative stimuli that 'everybody' understands. You must constantly envisage a type of reader if you want to play your tunes on his heart strings. How carefully Sheherazada, whose head depended upon it, studied her audience of one! How carefully the lady in Shaw's 'Man of Destiny' studies first the Lieutenant and then Napoleon, and fits her cozening tales to their psychology. It is so she makes her puppets dance.

But, says the poet, you admit I can only do this as far as the bits are concerned that I add to my poems. Now I write lyrics and so add very little, so your advice is worthless. But this is only in part true. Technical devices which in one poem have been employed by the conscious part of the poet's creative mechanism, in the next will probably have been handed on to his unconscious part. That is; the cunning of every artificer becomes in the end second nature. If this were not a fact, aesthetic theories would not be worth the ink in which they were set down.

Memory is apparently to a great extent under the jurisdiction of the subconscious part of our nature. What to-day we do with our wills, if it does not contradict some deep-seated desire in the subconscious, will to-morrow find itself adopted by the subconscious and coming out of it automaticallly. This is of course the foundation of all habit and of most sorts of technical skill.

It is, I think, in giving a reason for the consideration of his audience by the poet that the theory of art as communication developed in this book is chiefly useful. English literature has really suffered because we have always held a false aesthetic theory concerning the relations of poet and audience. The notion that the poet was there to create beauty, to pour forth his soul, has been the cause of a great deal of the gratuitous Goethic wildness that has spoiled so much of our literature. Writers of the Latin races have of course hardly suffered from this malady at all.

I have quoted Mr. Hueffer on this. As a student of Continental literature, he is acutely aware of the terrible way in which this lack of consideration for the reader has led English poets into a thousand faults. They maunder on through pages of dullness, they build 'huge heaps of littleness' in long meandering poems, they hide their treasure in a perfect jungle of false starts, bad similes, and discursive interludes, a jungle which a false aesthetic creed has made them too proud to prune. Consider Spenser's 'Faerie Queene,' consider the 'Duchess of Malfi,' consider 'Hamlet,' consider 'Clarissa,' consider 'Tristram Shandy,' and half of Scott's novels, and then think what a little Racineism, a little Volaireism in the way of form would have done for these half-buried pyramids of genius.

But, of course, once the poet has embarked on the idea that all he has to do is to create beauty and to express his soul, it is quite natural that he should turn with scorn from the idea of making his sublime creation agreeable to a reader. We cannot help feeling that there is something magnificent in this Gothicism, this turning from filthy lucre. Stevenson, who deliberately wrote to please, and learnt to subordinate his soul to that end, shows a little meanly by comparison with Wordsworth or Emily Brontë. But if we consider art as a means of communication, if we think how Spenser's or Richardson's literary self-indulgence has hindered the conveyance of their message, we shall I think, get a just view of the arts. The 'best-seller' Stevensonian point of view is a bad one because it is one that denies the value of the message to be conveyed, and we may compare the works of such writers to telephones in the hands of men who have nothing to say. On the other hand, the man who considers his inspiration as a thing holy and untouchable is like a man who has a message, but scorns the practical sordid telephone by which he might deliver it, and merely shouts it to the empty air.

If the reader thinks that this making of a fetish of the fruits of inspiration is a thing of the past I can, alas, assure him from personal experience that he is wrong. Every Editor of a Poetry Department will believe me when I say that I often get letters from writers in whose works I have ventured to suggest emendations, saying that they are aware that the passage complained of is a blemish, but that as it was part of the original inspiration, it is sacred and cannot be interfered with. I have two recent instances in mind. It is often difficult to convince such writers that the message to be conveyed may be sacred, but that the form in which it is to be conveyed is a matter, not of principle, but of commodity. It is not the form of words which is divine. Often a verbal formula will be inspired to its writer, when to a reader it is patent nonsense. Our dreams have surely allowed most of us to experience both sides of this. We have been both poet and auditor. The classical example is, of course, that of the philosopher who woke up in the middle of the night feeling that he had discovered the secret of the universe. Not trusting his memory in so vital a matter he took pencil and paper and wrote down the inspiration, feeling that in the morning the whole face of the world would be changed. When he woke up he found that he had written the following sentence, 'There are no differences but differences of degree between different degrees of difference and no difference.' After prolonged cogitation he was chagrined to have to admit that the statement was completely circular, and led nowhere. This, to my mind, does not, in itself disprove that he had for a moment in the middle of the night known the secret of the universe. What it does prove is the value of having as far as possible an efficient vehicle in which to convey ideas. His form of words proved a sieve incapable of containing the meaning which he had entrusted to it. There are quantities of poems like that. For poems for the most part deal with subtler things that are differences of 'degree.' However, in the literary works which we are considering, as 'Polyolbion,' or Spenser's 'Faerie Queene,' or 'The Excursion,' the problem is not quite like that of the dream formula, for the content has not here exactly leaked away (this is more characteristic of lyric poetry), it is merely that a jungle has made it impossible for the reader to get at it. To return to our original medical metaphor, the drug has been administered right enough, but in such a form, the opium embedded in such pounds of dough, the caffeine in such pints of milk, that it will probably pass through the body of the patient without affecting him in any way. The poet has got to consider what are the subsidiary drugs which, made up in the prescription, will enable his patient to digest and assimilate the principal drug. These assistant drugs are, of course, all the poetic devices which I have enumerated in previous chapters. First come recurring rhythyms, repetition, the alternate balancing and contrasting of allied but different ideas, and so on. All these are the rhythmic and incantational stock-in-trade of poetry, the devices by which certain too-insistent mental elements in the reader can be lulled to sleep. Secondly, we have the images, direct or associative, the symbols and comparisons by which the poet's ideas are conveyed to the system prepared by his rhythms.

Now though the reader is the more strongly affected and modified person of the two, he being the passive agent in the interchange of ideas, we shall find that the poet, largely because he is (or he would not be a poet) the more sensitive party, is very much affected by his audience and its attitude, and this side of the exchange I shall consider in the next chapter.

Chapter XII

THE POET AND HIS AUDIENCE

It has been the complaint of the old-fashioned of all ages that the young of their generation are addicted to coteries. Chaucer, Gower, and Dunbar were no doubt dubbed members of a Frenchified clique. Marlowe, Greene, Nash, and the rest formed a typical mutual admiration society. Dr. Johnson and Sir Joshua Reynolds were the leaders of a small urban club. The Lake poets were a close intimate corporation. The pre-Raphaelites wrote and painted for each other. The Georgians desire the praise of other Georgians; half the Cubists painted for Matisse or Piccasso, the other half for Mr. Roger Fry. Now this is as natural and as desirable as the division of the various portions of the human race into 'nations and languages.' Of all the inhabitants of the globe, there are at this moment perhaps about two hundred million people who read the English language. But the book which could be voluntarily read by them all would probably not be one which reached a very high level of art. Only a very simple love-story or cookery-book could in fact achieve half-an-hour's tolerance from such an audience, and a cookery-book which would please human beings from

Sutherlandshire *via* Sherry's in New York to the Malay States, would not be likely to thrill even one individual.

Misunderstanding is the begetter of dullness. The pound of butter would find five o'clock insufferably tedious. The best talk is the talk which springs up between intimates who have the same tastes, have seen the same places, and are familiar with the same authors. To the ill-informed upon any given subject you must speak of what is obvious—hence the penny Press. Therefore the artist who at all times seeks to pierce beyond the obvious may, nay, must address himself to the 'good listener' to whom the 'half-word,' the single stroke of the brush, which is sometimes all of the vision that he can bring back with him, will be significant.

Consider once more the case of Sheherazada. How curious it must have been to weave fancies for one only. If she knew what books the King had read, how allusive she could have been, how quickly have given him the shades of meaning she wanted, how easily have made him catch her points.

It would have seemed delightful for perhaps the first hundred of the thousand and one nights to address this coterie of one, for after the first five or six, she must have been thorough *en rápport* with him. But I should guess that after the first hundred, perhaps she began to find out the disadvantages of the coterie. For we cannot reduce even so good a thing as a coterie to the absurdity of a membership of one, without discovering that is has latent defects. Suppose the King was colour blind, or had never been any good at geography, or had a horror of insects, and utterly refused to listen to any similes about busy-bees and industrious ants? Sheherazada with her resourceful subtle mind must often have found that Pegasus flew with wings clipped, have longed for a wider public than the insatiable monarch provided—have felt a little as Henry James might have felt if he knew that his only auditors were the members of an Agricultural Workers' Union by whom his work was to be read and then burnt.

But if a coterie be of a fair size—a coterie to possess whose ear means that you must print your books, not circulate them in MS—then the poet can be perfectly happy in making use of all the knowledge that he may happen to possess. If Jones does not take his erudite comparison of the action of love to an ebb-tide with an off-shore wind, or alternatively to the action of Streptococcus, to a two-year-old filly in her first race, or to an *á priori* assumption, he can be sure that Smith or Robinson will. There will be someone in his audience who knows as much pathology as he does, who knows as much metaphysics as he does, who is even more of a nautical expert, or a racing man.

But, says the reader, now you are in effect arguing against the stifling effect of the coterie, and saying that the larger the audience the better, to which I reply that you have missed the point. These comparisons that our resourceful poet has made are only the trimmings on his poem. They are not absolutely essential to the comprehension of the word. What *is* essential is a certain standard of education, The poet must know that his audience are used to certain ideas. The more sensitive he is, the more he is likely to approximate his work to his estimation of his audience's intelligence, though not, of course, only to that of his immediate audience. An appeal to Posterity complicates the case of the poet. Mr. Lloyd George, the typical orator, catches the tone of whatever audience he may happen to be addressing. His Limehouse style was perfectly distinct from the style in which he addresses the House of Commons. That again is unlike that in which he speaks in Welsh to his local Welsh admirers. If we were to isolate him on several occasions before certain different types of audiences, by telling him that there were no reporters present, we should find that the character of those to whom he spoke affected his utterances still more markedly. So in a lesser degree is it with the poet. If he has a friend who he knows will read his work and this friend has an exquisite fancy and a fine taste, he will polish up the secondary conscious portions of his production with great care. The knowledge of this critical element in his audience will also, if his friend be kind and appreciative, at once restrain and enliven his subconscious creative process.

But, the poet may object: 'As a matter of fact, I do not write for any audience at all. I write because I have a sort of desire to write, or rather am conscious of acute discomfort if I do not write. I experience a kind of headache and write it off, much as I might try to walk off its physical counterpart. In practice, I never think of my audience. Your arguments are specious, but they do not accord with facts.'

Here I come to what is a little mental experiment with which I think I can prove my point that the audience does matter, even to the most superior and high-sniffing poet. Consider for a moment what would happen if, as a poet sat at his desk, there entered to him an old gentleman who offered to buy his entire output from now on for ever, and to pay a price more than generous for lyric, sonnet, epic, triolet and epigram, provided that he might burn every poem as he bought it, and that the poet promised to keep no copy. Suppose the poet was very hard up, and suppose that he agreed to this bargain. What would be the effect on his work? According to the theory that art is the highest form of self-expression and that the artist cares only for the finished product and nothing for potential readers, we should be obliged to say that it would have no effect at all and that the poet would continue to write and to polish with all his former care. He would probably console himself by showing each of his productions to a friend or two before the old gentleman called on Monday morning for the last week's output. But supposing one day the old gentleman discovered the poet's habit of Sunday night readings and—finger shaken in reproof of such subterfuge—refused to buy unless it were stopped. Suppose the poet to be still very poor. Suppose he again agrees. Would not the quality of his work very soon deteriorate? It would begin by his leaving an inappropriate epithet here and there, a discursive passage, an ill-thought out simile, but I think it would end with a rhyming dictionary and very little care except for the old gentleman's price. And supposing after a week or two of this, the old gentleman changed his terms a little and explained the purpose of his eccentric conduct to the young man. He held the belief that poetry was pernicious, that although produced by a set of worthy young men, yet it did in the world all the harm that the little boy had up before the magistrate attributes to the cinema. Hence he conceived himself as doing the greatest possible service to mankind in buying up and burning the products of a hundred facile pens. He visited in half a hundred houses round Oxford, was known to the porters of half-a-dozen colleges. What would the poet say to a contract? It must be a great deal of trouble to write so much verse and write it only to be burned, and his, the old gentleman's, end would be equally well served by a promise not to write any more.

'I have no objection to subsidising you. It is to your art, not your character that I object. Contract with me for a weekly sum, therefore, not to write any poetry. I demand nothing but your promise. Such an arrangement. I may point out, my young friend, would bring in the same financial return, and would give you leisure for those rational occupations for which the exercise of your poetic faculties at present gives you so little opportunity.'

Do you not think that after three weeks of indignant refusal the poet would agree? I think he would, and I think that if he were a real poet he would very soon retract his promise, repudiate the old gentleman and all his theories, refuse ever to see him again and begin to send his verse round to editors once more.

Now, if we accept the theory of art as a form of communication we shall not be bound, in believing this, to believe that the poet was not a sincere maker of beauty or that he was in search of praise or that he was in any way actuated by vain-glorious motives. The fact is that the poet is perpetually engaged in conjugating a transitive verb. He is an active agent in an exchange of ideas, but he and his readers ought never to forget that he is also a special, sensitized human being. Inevitably for different companies he will be a different person, he will write better for a wise than for a silly public. His audience, therefore, has a responsibility towards him. Not to take the trouble to understand his good work is as unfriendly in them, as it is to praise him when he writes badly. But this matter of praise and blame belongs more properly to the chapter on criticism, for, in my opinion, one of the chief duties of the critic is to act as spokesman for the else dumb public.

PART III

(FOR MISSIONARIES)

'Often the sexual instinct has a vast power over a boy's mind, because it means mystery and romance in a thoroughly prosaic world; and the world has become prosaic to him because all the desires of his spirit have been suppressed.'

DR. CRICHTON MILLER.

Chapter XIII

POETRY AND EDUCATION

A Committee, among whose members were Sir Henry Newbolt, Mr. John Bailey and Sir Arthur Quiller-Couch, was recently appointed by the President of the Board of Education

> 'To inquire into the position occupied by English (Language and Literature) in the educational system of England, and to advise how its study may best be promoted in schools of all types, including Continuation Schools, and in Universities and other Institutions of Higher Education, regard being had to:—
>
> (1) The requirements of a liberal education;
>
> (2) The needs of business, the professions, and public services, and
>
> (3) The relation of English to other studies.'

The Committee issued a report (*The Teaching of English in England.* London: H.M. Stationery Office, 1/6 net). This is a most enlightened document and really embraces the consideration of in how far the English language will serve as a vehicle for the humanities.

We all—except apparently Mme. Montessori—know the part which fairy tales and nursery rhymes play in the education of little children. They satisfy the child's appetite for beauty. In such things most children find their first aesthetic pleasure, and at the same time learn about such things as cats, cows, weddings and funerals, high mountains and deep rivers. But the same needs in the older child at school have not been very well understood or catered for.

But to return to the Committee. So wide were their terms of reference, that they came to the conclusion that they must decide what was meant by the term 'A liberal education,' and pronounce at large upon what were to be the aims of such a breeding:

> 'Education is not the same thing as information, nor does it deal with human knowledge as divided into so-called subjects. It is not the storing of compartments in the mind, but the development and training of faculties already existing. . . . It is, in a word, guidance in the acquiring of experience. Under this general term are included experiences of different kinds; those which are obtained, for example, by manual work, or by the orderly investigation of matter and its qualities. The most valuable for all purposes are those experiences of human relations which are gained by contact with human beings. . . . Education is complete in proportion as it includes within its scope a measure of knowledge in the principal sciences and a measure of skill in literature, the drama, music, song, and the plastic arts; but not all of these are equally useful for the training of the young. We recognise fully, on the one side, the moral, practical, educational value of natural science, on the other side the moral, practical, educational value of the arts and of all great literatures ancient or modern.'

What subject or what arrangement of curriculum will give us the best value?

'We make no comparison, we state what appears to us to be an incontrovertible primary fact, that for English children no form of knowledge can take precedence of the English Language and Literature: and that the two are so inextricably connected as to form the only basis possible for a national education.'

Most of those who are taking the trouble to read this book will probably not want to be persuaded that it is good for a child to be brought up in the love of good poetry, but in case one of the unconverted should have penetrated so far, I should like to say that I believe with the Committee who reported to the Board of Education that English literature is one of the best subjects for a child to study. But I also believe that a perfectly clear and reasoned case can be made out for the solemnest and most official inclusion of a study of the arts in any curriculum.

And here, as it seems to me, is one of the singularly few blemishes in an otherwise admirably-contrived treatise. The Committee never once quite face the arguments put forth by those who prefer music, one of the plastic arts, or perhaps the sciences as a means to culture. They seem particularly rather to forget that there are those who believe that the mind of a child is more easily approached through science. Mr. Sanderson, for example, shows in his flourishing public school at Oundle the complete working-model of a curriculum arranged from the opposite standpoint. Mental balance, clear thinking and intellectual disinterestedness are best taught through a study of the palpable wonders of the material world. Through Darwin, Pasteur, Newton and Einstein, say the advocates of this school, we can more easily widen a boy's horizon and teach him to think, than through Euripides, Shakespeare, Milton, Keats and Shaw. This is to many a new, and even a somewhat puzzling point, for it is only lately that the scientist has admitted the fact that his aims and those of the advocate of the Humanities are identical. Science has only just ceased to avow materialistic ends. To hear such a teacher as Mr. Sanderson enlarging almost in the words of the old pedagogues, upon the advantages of 'a sound, fortifying, scientific curriculum' merely for the formation of mind and character and for no immediate material end, is apt to prove a little bewildering.

The scientist has yet another point to make as far as literary expression is concerned and in bringing out Professor Aydelotte's theory he meets the humanist on his own ground. Professor Aydelotte, criticizing the curricula of a good many American Universities, protests vigorously against giving boys and girls what he calls 'the abstract gift of the gab.' Make boys and girls think, he urges, and in nine cases out of ten, if their thoughts are burning enough, the gift of expression will be added unto them.

This is, of course, our old friend the Owl and the Egg dilemma come back to haunt us. Is it the desire to express something that gives us the power of expression, or is it desire for self-expression that makes us seek for something to express? I believe, however, that this will not be found, on examination, to be quite so real a dilemma as it seems at first. The solution of it is, I think, to be sought in the region of a concept of the arts such as I tried to outline in Part II, that is as a very subtle form of communication between man and man. The reader may remember that the theory there expounded is roughly this:

We are each one of us shut into our private cell of individual sense perception. What may be called a direct statement—it may be conveyed in a statement in words, in a chemical formula, or in an algebraical equation—is a communication between one conscious intelligence and another conscious intelligence. An artistic statement—it may be one of Beethoven's posthumous Quartets, it may be a passage from *Early Intimations of Immortality*—is a communication both between one mind and another, and also between one subconsciousness and another. The arts are not, I believe, so much an expression of emotion as has been formerly thought —(the emotions are amphibious and may be conscious or subconscious)—but of the deeper substructure of the human mind. The artist's statement is the statement of what cannot be put 'into so many words.'

Though, therefore, it is conceivable (I am far from immediately admitting it) that the exact sciences form the more perfect medium by which one mind can understand another mind, yet in a curriculum based on the sciences the whole mental substructures are left out of account, and it is only in the domain of the arts that we find the entire nature of man brought into play.

A boy who has had a purely scientific education may find his will and mind beautifully trained, but I believe that he will find it much more difficult to manage his own character than the boy who has had his irrational impulses humanised through the arts. The scientifically brought up boy may have a noble conception of duty, a fine grasp of the theory of relativity, but some day he will fall in love, or suffer some other tremendous disturbance of the subconscious part of his nature. The whole of the curriculum which has educated his mind and his will has only served further to enslave, repress, and put out of sight the subconscious part of his being, and when it suddenly springs upon him like an armed man, he will not know what to do with it. Nothing in what he has learnt during the time when, for instance, the sex impulse was reasonably manageable has now any bearing upon the struggle which he has to go through. At best his training will have given him such tremendous control over his subconscious powers—will have so stiffened the repressing element in him—that his character will not suffer shipwreck, but even in this case, he will be losing his energies in a conflict which, if he had humanised the forces within him, might have been unnecessary. Mr. Sanderson is well aware how necessary it is that a school curriculum should, above all, fit a boy to live with his fellows and to understand them, and a very good understanding his scholars get of the whole of the rational side of human nature. If strikes were always caused by low wages and bad houses; if wars were always caused by the tyranny of a ruler, or some purely economic condition; if the laws of political economy were not eternally cut across by the laws of human psychology, then Mr. Sanderson's pupils would be well-equipped indeed. But let us take a fantastical example, I think that a child brought up exclusively on Mr. de la Mare's poetry would have a better chance of understanding his fellows' rare rational behaviour, than a boy educated solely through science would have of understanding their irrational behaviour.

It is on such grounds that the humanist should, I hold, base his claim against the scientist. It is on these grounds that he can maintain that through the humanities men can best reach that state of mutual understanding, sympathy and co-operation which, were it achieved, would so nearly bring us to the state of an earthly paradise. But upon this side of the question the compilers of the Report have not touched even briefly, and those who are inclined to believe in the approach to a civilised character and a developed intelligence through the sciences may find themselves a little antagonised by a merely tacit assumption that everyone acknowledges that we can approach culture best through the arts; by being brought into contact, that is, with other and great minds rather than with marvellous and stimulating facts.

But in this book we are not considering the case of the arts or even literature in general, but of poetry in particular, and there still remains the minor question of why we should try to teach children to love poetry rather than one of the other arts. Here I should like to put forward one argument and one only, which is the argument of sheer brute convenience. There is only one art of which we can be sure that its practice and enjoyment can be pursued by all the children whom we endeavour to equip for the world, in whatever situation they may find themselves. Life on a South Sea Island, or in an oasis in the Sahara, or at sea, or in Hull, or in Pernambuco, will make it impossible for the painter, the musician, the amateur of ballet or the drama to enjoy his particular form of art. A Medici print and a gramophone enable him to practice with but sadly 'maimèd rights.' But the man who loves poetry can nearly everywhere contrive a pencil, a pad of paper and a shelf of books.

Again from the teaching aspect in the case of national education (the aspect dealt with in the Report)—the argument of brute convenience—comes in once more. We have to deal with millions of children, we cannot, alas, just now afford to supply them with elaborate tools and instruments: we cannot even easily give them the necessary space in which to cultivate such arts as painting and dancing, therefore the arts of literature and poetry again seem our readiest tools.

How can we best give children cause to love poetry? For in the words of Ben Jonson, 'A youth should not be made to hate study before he know the cause to love it.' There are, of course, a number of admirable text books to be had on teaching children to write English, in which the reasons for the condemnation of the 'composition' and the school 'essay' are set out. We are here to seek for the forms of literary expression along the lines of what young children would choose for themselves if left alone. Some quite primitive form will please them best, and it is now usual to begin the young author with that most primitive form of all—the story, not written, but told. The composition and the essay both have their counterpart in the companion art of learning to read good literature. It used to be—alas! it still is in many schools—the custom to go through a play of Shakespeare's a term. By the old system the soul-shaking, breath-taking story of Macbeth is interrupted for the parsing of special passages, or a discussion as to whether the crow flew to Rooky or to Rocky Woods. This method is of course absolutely fatal. The modern method is to let children in school read as grown-up people do, quickly and currently, with occasional skipping and occasional ignoring of difficult passages. But granted a common-sense method, there still remains a practical question, What poetry should be put into the hands of children? This question I propose to discuss in the next chapter.

Chapter XIV

POETRY AND THE CHILD

'Adult life is the antithesis of the nursery in many respects, but it resembles it in this: that it is still a narrow territory of familiar things on the edge of a great expanse of unknown country.'

Dr. Crichton Miller.

In body, mind and desires the child of six differs completely from the child of eleven, and the child of eleven from the boy or girl of sixteen. These differences are not superficial, they seem to extend down to the depths of the child's nature. Poetry is concerned with fundamental things, and, therefore, if we are trying to provide a child with a poetic diet, it is no good ignoring or slurring over these universal age-made differences. In its relation to poetry I think we might divide childhood into four ages—the Age of Enchanment up to about seven or eight; the Age of Reason from eight to twelve or even fourteen. This merges into the Ethical Age lasting till adolescence brings the Age of Love.

Would any poetic missionary who reads this chapter please note that he will find plenty of adults whose poetical appreciation has stuck in one or other of these categories.

I

How early can we begin to read poetry to children, how soon will they be ready? The answer, of course, depends on your definition of poetry. Mine emphatically includes 'Hey, diddle, diddle,' and "Pat a cake, pat a cake,' and 'Leg over, Leg over,' also 'Over the Hills and Far Away' and 'Here we dance, Looby.' I therefore should give the age as about nine months to a year. The child seems to find in this sort of poetry, in pure colour and simple tunes, its first aesthetic experiences, and poetic rhythms are often popular before the child can speak or apparently understand. But leaving Nursery Rhymes aside—in a proper house the child will absorb them naturally—I found that my two daughters when aged two and three and a half, developed a taste for Mr. de la Mare's poems, three and a half repeating :—

> 'Ann, Ann !
> Come ! quick as you can,
> There's a fish that *talks*
> In the frying pan,
>   Out of the fat,
>   As clear as glass
>   He put up his mouth,
>   And moaned "Alas ! "
>   Oh, most mournful,
>   "Alas, Alack,"
>   Then turned to his sizzling,
>   And sank him back.'

Two years old was almost overcome by the pathos of this. Rather to my surprise no less popular was the highly metaphysical :—

> 'Do diddle di do,
>   Poor Jim Jay
> Got stuck fast
>   In Yesterday.
> Squinting he was,
>   On cross-legs bent,
> Never heeding
>   The wind was spent.
> Round veered the weathercock,
>   The sun drew in—
> And stuck was Jim
>   Like a rusty pin . . .'

I always dreaded a day when I should be asked for a rational explanation of this poem, but I am thankful to say that the glamour of the conception, or the swing of the metre carried us all over the danger.

In poems of pure imagination, I noticed a marked difference between two and three, three-years-old being immensely impressed by :—

> 'Someone came knocking
>   At my wee, small door;
> Someone came knocking,
>   I'm sure-sure-sure; . . .'

while two-years did not care for it. The poems in Miss Rose Fyleman's *The Fairy Flute* were enjoyed by three years old. She insisted upon having the whole book read to her backwards and forwards, over and over again—swallowing the good and the bad together. There are some very bad poems in Miss Fyleman's book, poems that are all that verse for children ought not to be, to set off the charm of, ‘If you meet a Fairy.’

On the whole, however, traditional poems or poems by very ‘expert’ mystics will be what children up to six or seven will like best. Who has not noticed the imaginative child’s preference for the ‘old favourites,’ *i.e.* the traditional fairy tales. This, I believe, is neither fortuitous nor the result of conservatism. The child, even if it has not got a definite racial memory (the assertion that it has is often made but seems to me not proved), at least responds distinctly, more readily to primitive than to ‘made-up’ symbolism. The traditional fairy tale and nursery rhyme employ the real dream symbolism. We shall come across the magic Bull, the Cross-road, the Bridge, the Serpent, the Deep River, the Dark Forest. Wolf and Witch stand for the powers of evil; the Prince or Princess suffer metamorphorsis into small impotent creatures; space is subject to such devices as seven league boot; the chronology is dream chronology. Then in ‘The Tanglewood Tales’ the seasonal gods and nature myths seem to strike an easy response. But now and then the modern expert mystic obviously manages to ‘strike on the same matchbox.’ Edward Lear’s *Nonsense Book*, ‘Peacock Pye,’ and ‘Alice in Wonderland’ would, I think, be instinctively classed with ‘The Three Sillies,’ ‘The Sleeping Beauty’ and ‘Childe Roland’ by any intelligent child. Mr. de la Mare’s poems, some of Blake’s *Songs of Innocence*, Stevenson’s *Child’s Garden of Verses*, and every sort of legend and traditional tale is the diet for this age.

II

The child ultimately emerges from the Age of Enchantment—the age of 'The King of Spain's Daughter,' 'The Seven Champions of Christendom,' 'Bre'er Wolf,' of Dis, Prosepine and Pandora. When it is between eight and twelve, shades of the prison house will have begun to close—the age of reason has set in, to last till adolescence brings a fresh age of vision. We shall not only have to feed the child on different poetic food, but we may very likely have to justify our own aesthetic creeds before the child's understanding. He or she has begun to ratiocinate, and we generally find that a developing reason is employed like the new three-bladed knife—it is tried upon every substance with which its owner comes into contact. It is a rather destructive, or, if you prefer it, an efficient analytical weapon.

Who was it who said that both the aim and the method of education could be summed up as 'the effort to make a child inquisitive and keep it so?' If the child has been properly brought up, and has a rightly enquiring mind, he will, as soon as he enters this, the angular age, begin to ask awkward fundamental questions about aesthetics. One hideous point he is sure to bring up, probably towards the latter part of this period, 'How can you prove that it is "better" to admire Leonardo, Augustus John and Flecker, rather than Leader, Landseer, Longfellow, and Ella Wheeler Wilcox?' I am not sure that the cross-examined elder had not better admit at once that he cannot prove the superiority of good art, but can only make it seem probable. How? It is no good to talk about communication and the subconsciousness to an urchin. The most effective set of arguments that I know in the favour of good art is that summarised by Mr. John Bailey, in an Eton Ephemeral which appeared during the War, called, I think along with several rivals or successors, 'The Red Cross.' He began by saying that in cricket or in football we were ready to take the word of those who had given the most serious attention to the game. In matters of style, if we were not ourselves notable players we deferred to acknowledged experts. Would readers grant to him the same principle in the arts?—grant that on the whole and in all probability, those who gave most time and attention to aesthetics, that is, poets, painters, critics, and connoisseurs were likely to understand more about the subjects of their studies than could those who gave the arts a thought now and then that they could spare from other business? If the evidence of these expert witnesses were to be given the special weight that we should give to that of professionals in any other sphere then we had very good evidence on which to base the assertion that Beethoven was a better musician than the composer of 'Where my caravan has rested.' It would probably be difficult to find one lifelong student of music to come forward and uphold the superiority of the latter, whereas it would be easy enough to produce a dozen expert witnesses in favour of Beethoven.

Also, good art, be it music, painting, or poetry, produces a very vivid sort of pleasure in its votaries. This pleasure has not got a very satisfactory name. It has often been called aesthetic ecstacy. When we are at the 'receiving end' of a good piece of art we experience an intense, vivid delight, we are lifted out of ourselves, our stature is increased, the beauty of a picture may half intoxicate us, the poignancy of a play or of a poem may be almost unbearably vivid. But those who burn candles at lesser altars, never experience anything more intense than a slight feeling of pleasure and gratification. They know a passing satisfaction in their Hawaian walse, their 'Monarch of the Glen,' their 'Beautiful Valley of Death,' their 'Chu Chin Chow,' but that is all. Only the best art can ultimately 'deliver the goods.'

Mr. Bailey, therefore, leaves us, if not with an absolute proof of the superiority of 'good art,' at least with two strong arguments to make in its favour. First, the claims of expert witnesses, secondly, the argument of degrees of pleasure.

I personally think that in putting all this forward to the enquiring child, we ought to qualify and hedge to the extent of saying that it is often in pratice difficult to divide art into true and spurious. We must beware of aesthetic snobbery. If we look close enough, the difference between good and bad is here of degree, not of kind. We are presented with a white shading to black, and it is perhaps doubtful if we can find any absolute white works of art while absolute black works of art are also rare. It is especially no condemnation of a tune or verse or picture that it is popular. Sir Edwin Lutyens' cenotaph is a case in point. There were a dozen songs that were intensely beloved in the War which had considerable elements of charm. I refuse to take up a superior attitude to 'I do like to be beside the seaside.' I consider 'Pack up your troubles' keeps well this side of sentimentality, and I find something rather splendid in its simplicity. 'I want to go home' is patchy, but strikes in general a note of satire and melancholy humour most effectively. And if we must discriminate in favour of what are generally esteemed as 'black works of art,' we must do the same for the white pieces. A good many readers are intensely bored by Tennyson and Wordsworth, and in nine cases out of ten, they have much reason on their side. They have probably been introduced to these poets in the wrong way, and have started upon the wrong poems. They do not know of the existence of the kernel, and can hardly be blamed for finding the shell hard and tough. The child from eight to twelve or fourteen is a natural iconclast. Let us be frank with him, and give him leave to make an Aunt Sally of dull or pretentious poems whoever may have written them.

I said we should have to change the child's poetic food about this time. What shall we find will now best satisfy his appetite? His mental change has been towards rationalism, and away from imaginative things. We shall find, therefore, that when he desires to experience the pleasures of the fancy as he still will, he will need enormous doses of those anodynes with which in poetry we lull the too-insistent logical and analytical faculties.

I, at about twelve or thirteen years, and a boy whose poetic mentor I was, had, I remember for our favourites, 'The Lady of Shalott,' 'When we Two Parted in Silence and Tears,' 'Come not when I am dead,' 'Break, break,' some of the songs from 'The Faithful Shepherdess,' 'The Isles of Greece,' 'Tears, Idle Tears,' and passages from Milton such as 'Whom the Almighty Power.' This choice showed, I think, that what we wanted were insistent rhythms, melodramatic or slightly sugary sentiment, and the greatest possible gorgeousness of language.

This was our choice in matters of lyrics. By way of long poems we used to read modernisations of the Icelandic Sagas, we tolerated 'Hiawatha,' we liked 'The Siege of Lucknow,' and 'The Revenge.' I think 'The Charge of the Light Brigade' slightly stuck in our throats, but perhaps we were rather sophisticated children. In narrative, next to our love of fighting and battles came our love of anything that made our flesh creep. I remember learning Browning's 'In a Laboratory' by heart and acting it, also most of Rossetti's 'Sister Helen':

'Oh, the waxen knave was plump to-day,
Sister Helen;
How like dead folk he has dropped away!'
Nay how, of the dead what can you say,
Little Brother?
*(Oh, Mother, Mary Mother,
What of the dead, between Hell and Heaven?)*'

I think that 'Christabel' was a little too good for us, though we delighted in the shorter and more rhythmically insistent 'Kubla Khan.' But I remember how the age of reason boggled at 'The Toothless Bitch' who bayed so punctually—like the cook's alarm clock. During the dry, Voltairian age of reason and curiosity, the only form of sustenance powerful enough to reach the almost buried imagination is, in fact, generally melodrama—that is violent emotion set to insistent rhythms.

III

After this most children go through a metaphysical stage, the transition is marked by taking to 'Macbeth' and 'Samson Agonistes.' We become priggish and read 'Marcus Aurelius.' Then is the time for the missionary to introduce the young person to Emily Brontë's 'The Old Stoic,' to Wordsworth's 'Happy Warrior,' to 'Early Intimations of Immortality,' 'Ode to Duty,' and perhaps to 'Simon Lee, the Old Huntsman.'

Some boys and girls like Crabbe at this age, and about now I should introduce a little Masefield into the diet, for instance, 'The River' and 'The Wanderer.' With some young people and the children of some parents, also 'Daffodil Fields' and 'The Everlasting Mercy.' Mr. Gordon Bottomley's 'King Lear's Wife,' and 'Britain's Daughter' would please this age, a great deal of Dryden, and perhaps Pope. The amount of didacticism that I could then lap up amazes me.

IV

Not till adolescence is complete should we try to get the girl or boy to enjoy love poetry. There will come spring when you will find your pupil spontaneously deep in it.

> 'All thoughts, all passions, all delights,
> Whatever stirs this mortal frame,
> All are but ministers of Love,
> And feed his sacred flame.'

His soul will tremble to the enchantment of 'Endymion.' If your pupil is a girl don't let her at this stage read for the first time 'Hero and Leander,' 'Venus and Adonis,' Mr. Aldous Huxley's 'Leda,' or even 'The Maid's Tragedy.' If she has read them before, and is familiar with them, it will be all right, but I solemnly believe and aver that there are two or three years at least in a girl's life when these poems read for the first time, possess a real power to wound and to freeze the opening flower.

Let the girl be as sentimental as she likes about love. If a girl child is a great reader, and will not be warned, and has a library at her command, then look ahead and see to it that she reads Don Juan early. Such poems act on many natures not provocatively, but like a cold wind. Such a wind may be harmless when the tree is in bud, and wholesome when the fruit is set, but there is a short time when the blossom may be hurt by it, when only the soft airs of Keats and Spencer should blow.

Chapter XV

LEARNING TO READ POETRY

I THINK most children understand what they are to expect from poetry almost automatically, and if we try explanation and poetical theory with them, we shall probably only darken counsel and make puzzling what was before perfectly clear. But in the case of grown-up beginners, or even beginners in their late teens, the missionary ought, I think, to give the Reason a general sort of idea of what it is that we expect from poetry. As we get older our appreciative faculties decrease and our analytical, critical and comparative faculties increase. Thus (as long as we have not been bored by long discourses) of all the things we have learned as adults, we enjoy best what we understand best.

Mr. J. F. Roxburgh's 'Poetic Procession' is a brilliant little pamphlet intended as a beginners' introduction to English poetry, and made up from two lectures delivered to working men. The pamphlet consists of about fifty pages of fairly large printing, and not only does Mr. Roxburgh have to give in it a sort of lightning impression of half a dozen individual poets and as many epochs, but from the method he has employed he is obliged to set out very briefly what are the qualities which we look for in poetry. This is obviously not only a thing which it is impossible to do completely, but which it is difficult to do even partially without recourse to talk of over and upper meaning and the hypnotic effects of recurring rhythms and of rhymes, and of the metaphorical basis of language. All these 'aids to reflection' were denied him by the nature of the audience to which he was addressing himself; but he does remarkably well with what is left to him, saying very simply that 'what poetry does for us is to give us new ideas, clearer visions, stronger emotions, and also to express as we could not have done for ourselves what we have already thought and seen and felt.' Incidentally the pamphlet is full of amusing epigrams about poets and periods:—'Milton is,' he says 'the poet of black and white.' Wordsworth appealed to the heart and the senses; Coleridge to the imagination. 'With Wordsworth it is always Sunday: with Byron it is never Sunday.'

Had I an audience of adults to convince—an audience not stupid, but bred, say, as commercial travellers or analytical chemists—I should be very much inclined to make an experiment. I should begin by trying to express partly in words of one syllable, partly in parable, the theories set out in this book about poetry as a means of communication between two subconsciousnesses, stressing especially the notion that by means of art you can express just those things that you cannot put into so many words, and in this connection I should relate an anecdote—quoted as a matter of fact by Mr. Roxburgh in a different connection :—'When Byron was at Trinity, Cambridge, it is said that he bought a large black bear, dressed it in cap and gown, and introduced it to the Dean.' Imagine the miserable crudeness of an attempt to express this piece of satire by direct statement! Then I should give some examples of satiric and comic poetry and of epigrams, pointing out the conciseness given by the poetic form, and the way in which a poet is able to direct the reader's attention to particular points by means of the devices of emphasis which he is able to wield (such as rhyming on a word the reader is to notice, using the accented part of the line, and so forth). Presently, after my audience were soothed in their reasons by so much that sounded 'sensible' I should go on to speak of true poetry, and here I should be very much inclined not so much as to mention the 'old masters' at all—Keats, Milton, Shelley, Shakespeare, and the rest. It is possible even probable that the child's mind is really most familiar with what is most remote, but I should first try to win adults to an appreciation of modern poetry, and I should consider the usual 'standard poets' purely as an advanced course. I should nurse my hearers up on Brooke, Shanks, Masefield, Robert Nicholls, Siegfried Sassoon, the Sitwells, and so on. All this modern work is near to them, for, as Mr. Roxburgh remarks, 'among other things the modern movement is a movement which is bringing poetry considerably closer to everyday life.' Now an adult beginner would probably start in what we might call a utilitarian frame of mind: the attitude that asks 'What will poetry do for me?' and therefore this nearness to everyday life might be a very valuable quality in our 'didactic material.'

Take the case of love poetry, for instance. I believe it is a comparatively mature taste that wants to read of the loves of Aeneas, of the face that launched a thousand ships, of Cleopatra and her worm, and a still maturer that can bear the abstraction of Chloe, Daphnis and Strephon.

I would far sooner confront my commercial travellers and my 'tired business men' with Mr. D. H. Lawrence's 'If I never see her again' or Miss Mew's 'Madeleine in Church,' or some love poem of Rupert Brooke's. One of the easiest methods of showing what poetry is and what it does, is to contrast it with prose, and for this purpose it is very much easier to use Miss Sitwell's poem about the tram, than a passage, say, from Tennyson's 'Princess.'

I should regard some of Mr. Masefield's poems as very strong cards. Take, for example, some of the passages in 'Right Royal,' describing the racing crowd: The groom with the face like yellow parchment, the bookies, the wagonette from 'The Old Pier Head,' or this charming neat piece of work:—

'The costermongers as smart as sparrows
Brought their wives in their donkey barrows.
The clean-legged donkeys, clever and cunning,
Their ears cocked forward, their neat feet running,
Their carts and harness flapping with flags,
Were bright as heralds and proud as stags.

And there in pride in the flapping banners
Were the costers' selves in blue bandanas,
And the costers' wives in feathers curling,
And their sons, with their sweet mouth-organs skirling.'

From this I should be able to bring them on insensibly, a feeling of firm ground still under their feet, to more imaginative passages in 'Dauber' and perhaps even to the climax of 'The Everlasting Mercy.' For the purpose of general leading on, war poems are very useful, the violence of Mr. Sassoon's war poems not less than Mr. Masefield's beautiful elergy, 'August 1914.' Perhaps here one might begin with William Wilfred Gibson's dying soldier who goes on planning his allotment:—

'Two rows of cabbages,
Two of curly-greens,
Two rows of early peas,
Two of kidney beans.'

or perhaps the following, from 'Neighbours':—

'Stripped mother-naked except for a gold ring,
Where all day long the gaping doctors sit
Decreeing life or death, he proudly passed
In his young manhood; and they found him fit.

Of all that lustiness of flesh and blood
The crash of death has not left anything,
But tumbled somewhere in the Flanders' mire
Unbroken lies the golden wedding-ring.'

Then one might go on with one of Mr. Sassoon's rather horrific verses, and round all off with 'Everyone Singing' or a verse or two from 'August 1914.' Such examples, so treated, would I honestly believe prove the conversion of many, for we all know some aspect of the emotional significance of the war. We all know that this emotion is no hoax of the poets, but something which we ourselves know—something which, moreover, could not be expressed in a telegram. So that in the instance of war poetry our task is made easier by the fact that we have only got to sort the good from the bad. We shall here find our main argument, 'Say it in verse,' accepted, and we have left remaining only the less nebulous and therefore easier task of leading our scholars on to a preference for good verse.

It is at this stage that I should introduce some of my examples of how not to do it, for this is a weapon in whose efficiency I have great faith. Heaven knows, there is no lack of bad war poetry! We shall easily find bellicose verse about the Hun being at the gate and our sword being unsheathed (here the rhymes will be gate, fate, hate). We could quote sentimental verses on the non-return of Daddy (mild, child, fay, play); verses about ministering angels in hospitals, about 'cheery' wounded (fag will rhyme with flag). There will be verses to remind us of Campbell's 'Wounded Hussar.' Does the reader recollect this? It is one of the best pieces in my private 'Tin Treasury':

> 'Alone to the bank of the dark-rolling Danube
> Fair Adelaide hied when the battle was o'er:—
> "Oh, whither," she cried, "hast thou wandered, my lover?
> Or here dost thou welter and bleed on the shore?

What voice did I hear? 'Twas my Henry that sighed?"
All mournful she hastened, nor wandered she far,
When bleeding, and low, on the heath she descried,
By the light of the moon her poor wounded Hussar!'

With this 'explosion of all the upholsterers' I should contrast another 'humanitarian' war poem:

'Ah, were I King of Spain,
Or better, Pope of Rome,
I'd have no fighting men abroad,
No weeping maids at home.'

I am sure that the old-fashioned advertisers were right. There is nothing so effective as the two pictures of the man 'Before taking Nurse Trumpington's word-famed drops, and after.' Particularly is the method useful in the arts. For in trying to pass on our own pleasure, we must never forget the limitations of criticism, and chiefly that prime limitation which I have tried to prove—the fact that the whole point of the content of the arts is that you cannot express it in a direct statement. That is why, especially to a non-adept audience, example is finally worth more than precept. Though I believe that, adult man being a rational creature, precept also has its place because it meets the interruptions and objections of the ratiocinating part of his nature. Again, if you teach largely by giving examples, the reader has not got to take all the points on your 'say so.' The almost infinite badness of 'fair Adelaide' sticks out quite obviously. But we must be ambitious and take popular favourites in this way. We may find it rather more difficult to explain what is wrong with some of Ella

Wheeler Wilcox's poems. They have a curious unnerving vigour. Perhaps the best way of exposing her faults is to contrast some poem of hers with a good poem, if possible upon the same subject, or, her subjects being most strangely chosen, if the missionary's ingenuity does not run to this, then at any rate with a poem which strives to attain the same emotional effect.

II.

There is a question which is sometimes asked by those who would like to like poetry, and that is whether it is a good thing to learn by heart? I think most emphatically that it is, but the learner must be very careful in the choice of his piece. It must be something that he really likes, that has really struck his imagination; he must feel that he would like to live with it, must choose it as if he were choosing a wife.

Another conundrum. We may be asked to define poetry, to draw the line between poetry and prose. This is, of course, quite impossible, but the question at least gives us a text for impressing on our readers that it is the spirit, the intention, that makes poetry, not the letter, and that a metrical arrangement of words is only the method by which poetry usually seeks to attain certain ends. But verse is no more necessarily poetry than a non-metrical arrangement is necessarily prose.

'Thirty days hath September,
April, June, and November,
All the rest have thirty-one
Excepting February alone,
Which has but twenty-eight days clear
And twenty-nine in each Leap Year.'

Vers libre, polyphonic prose and prose proper, are all forms which shade into one another. There is no question of merit—Abraham Lincoln's Gettysburg speech and Second Inaugural are both true prose; 'Dream Fugues,' 'Urn Burial,' 'Can Grande's Castle' we might take as representing polyphonic prose. Some of Mr. Richard Aldington's Free Verse or Mr. Squire's poem about the football match are both in the next stage, and though here and there using a prose rythm, have begun to be printed like verse. And so on, and so on, until we get by minute stages to such verse as:

'There be none of Beauty's daughters
With a magic like to thee,
And like music on the waters
Is thy sweet voice to me:'

We might here indeed take an analogy from the kitchen. The nature of the poem, as of the jelly or the blanc-mange, remains unchanged whether it is put into a mould representing a hedgehog, or turned out of a pudding basin, or broken up into glasses. Some people complain that if, in shape, it is to represent a bird or an elephant, the cook is likely to make it too stiff. On the other hand, the non-expert guest, who does not know what excellent things have gone into the mixture, may be distressed by having it served to him in a form to which he is not accustomed.

Last of all, I should try and warn my audience against what I believe to be a pernicious fallacy, and that is that the object of cultivating the taste is to become more austere. Austerity is at best a negative virtue. Matthew Arnold says: 'We must accustom ourselves to a high standard and to a strict judgment, and thus learn to recognise the best in poetry.' Mr. Sturge Moore agrees with him. 'We must maintain,' he says, 'a determination to become only intimate with verse that stands the test of our most active moods, instead of letting the luckless day, with its relaxed temper, console itself with something that we have perceived to be second-rate. For in proportion as we are loyal to our taste, it will become more difficult to please, until at last a really sound judgment is acquired.' He goes on still further to identify good taste with being hard to please and its cultivation as an eradication of bad habits of mind. I believe that this is all nonsense. Try and find out what is liked by people whose judgment you trust, if at first you don't like it yourself; try to find out what they see in the particular author or passage, but never set out to try and dislike even fustian. I believe there is something automatically 'refining' in the best examples of art, and that if we can care for two or three really good poems for themselves and not for any adventitious reason, that will automatically make us dissatisfied with 'fake poetry.' And after all, what if we were to get pleasure from the second-rate? True the public has a duty to the poets who write for it, and we ought to try to distinguish between the good and the bad; but admiration is to some extent a Fortunatus' purse, and in admiring something which is perhaps not strictly worthy of admiration, we are not necessarily robbing some other poet of his rightful heritage. In this matter of praise and appreciation it is as true as it is in the world of law, that it is better to let off two or three guilty prisoners, than to condemn one innocent one. It is better to overpraise a few earnest but mediocre souls than to underpraise one Keats.

Chapter XVI

LEARNING TO WRITE POETRY

In these days of poetic liberty we desire an oblique glimpse of something exquisite rather than the flawless statement of the commonplace. But even in this happy epoch there remains the yard-stick. Mr. Munro and Mr. Squire, and in a less degree Mr. Middleton Murry, are exceedingly sure of the complete accuracy and efficacy of their measures. They are also quite sure that below a certain rather high standard of proficiency it is better not to write, and it is sinful to publish. Possibly they are right. The standard of technical ability, both in prose and verse, is low in England—much lower than in France, for instance. Our young poets—those who are most promising—are often the better for a good 'head-masterish' talking to. Many of them need a fright which will lead them in future to take greater pains with their verses before they ask the durability of printers' ink for them. But let us remember the parable of the Wheat and the Tares. The householder was so anxious that the good seed should not be rooted up and spoilt that he was very lenient with the weeds. Such, it seems to me, should be the attitude of the critic. The stream of bad verse which pours weekly from a thousand pens is, after all, a negative evil. Keats said the last word about a beautiful thing. One beautiful poem is a positive good—a palpable new jewel for the public treasury. It more than cancels out the ninety and nine.

Poets are as various as their works, and there is probably no general piece of advice as to the writing of verse that can be given even to young poets. Perhaps a few concrete examples of do's and dont's illustrated by poems sent in in the ordinary way to *The Spectator* may be of use to the beginner—to whom alone this chapter is addressed.

Two or three poets have been kind enough to allow me to give, as samples of several varying grades in the art of poetic proficiency, verses which they have submitted to *The Spectator* for publication. The first is a slight lyric, ' Moon ' :

' Long years ago the moon,
  When earth was flame,
  Left his embrace and came
Out to the arms of space,
Hiding for shame her face.

Earth, when she fled, grew cold,
  Mourned her with tears in vain,
But still as the seasons pass,
  Love draws the twain :
Earth strives again to hold
Moon, till she hides her face,
  Fearing love's pain.'

The first verse is agreeable and the notion attractive, but in the second verse we feel that the expression of the thought is manufactured. Now the first verse could not stand alone, so the poet completed his work as best he could. All poets inevitably fill up faults or cracks with inferior material to some extent. But we have to consider the proportion of primary and secondary matter and the workmanship of the pedestrian parts. In 'Moon' there are seven clay lines to five golden, and the faultiness of the last two lines is obvious.

A poem on autumn by the same author has very good points, despite a line which necessitates 'sad-*den*ing.' But it has good lines in it—for example, despite its more than doubtful ornithology: —

> 'All birds are silent, crouching in their nests,
> Rain-soaked and tossed unending by the wind.'

An effect of dripping melancholy is well achieved and maintained.

There is another poem on autumn in the collection. The first fault I have to find with this is that it consists of seven verses, while the idea of the thing could have been expressed in about four. In the second verse we find ''tis autumn.' Then in verse three :—

> 'The leaves fall softly, red and brown,
> And now and then a chestnut ripe
> Few of God's choir seem now to pipe.
> The yearly sands are running down.
> And all is beautiful . . .'

'Few of God's choir seem now to pipe' is obviously bad. It is quite out of keeping with a poem which set out to be a visualization—a fairly realistic picture. To call birds 'God's choir' belongs to a different imaginative 'layer'; and though it might conceivably be introduced effectively where a completely fresh turn was to be given to a poem, it certainly must not be vaguely set in like that. 'The yearly sands are running down' 'And all is beautiful' are two disconnected ideas very unhappily married. Later on the poet asks, What is the meaning of all this gentle beauty?

'. . . Need we ask?
To answer is an easy task.
Earth hears Death's footstep on the stair.'

We thought we were out of doors—what stair? As for verse seven, it is too weak to endure the torture of dissection. I pass on to a more robust victim.

Here is another long poem, 'Legerdemain.' Its author is about eighteen :—

'The Old Man of Dreams bore me, pickaback,
Clasping his shoulders bent with magic sack.'

The Old Man takes the narrator in this metre to the end of the world where stars are made. There sits Time, mighty, on a throne of fire : the Hours frolic round him. The Hours sing :—

'Men shall always woo us
(We care not for their love or hate).
They think that they may bind us
(We fashion their sorry fate) . . .'

The jolt is really atrocious, for the object of introducing short line lyrics into the middle of a narrative poem is surely to produce a musical effect; to edge, as it were, further away from the prose-characteristics that the narrative necessitated. Limping lines are here, therefore, unforgiveable, and in this lyric, which consists altogether of eight lines, there are no fewer than four lame ones. But to continue. An Hour goes weeping to Time, saying she is lost: she has not performed her appointed watch on earth and has missed her turn. Then the poet commits the hideous mistake of making Time rise from his throne, whereas before, his description had given us quite a pleasing, Blakeian idea of Time as a vast elemental creature whose top reached to the heavens and his feet to the ends of the earth. But when he stands to address the meeting he dwindles. There follows an obscure verse in which the poet, prompted by the Old Man of Dreams, consents to take the Hour for his bride, and we end with the poet somewhat entangled in his metaphor. It is impossible to make sure whether the Hour does or does not change from a personification to a subdivision of Time during which the poet may consider the charms of an earthly beloved.

I apologize to the authors of these poems for dissecting their mistakes and disregarding their virtues.

Young poets very often write to me for advice. They send me their entire life's work, or their relations do, and ask me 'to class these 60 poems in order of merit, A, B or C.' I don't know that my advice is ever any good. As a rule I refer them to some good books of criticism—very often Mrs. Wilkinson's 'New Voices' and Mr. Sturge Moore's 'Some Soldier Poets,' and, if I think their work is inclined to be 'soppy,' to Mr. Harold Munro's 'Some Contemporary Poets, 1920.' To the more intelligent and promising I should now also, of course, always recommend Mr. Graves' new book 'On English Poetry.'

I have been looking through the rather dreary records of the advice that I have given. A good many people I seem to have accused of sitting down to write poetry, rather than trying to express any very vivid thought or emotion, the consequence being the production of a mild type of work without any very active faults, but which does not seem particularly worth writing. A poet who got a certain amount of emotion into his verse was not careful of his words, and at regular intervals introduced a cliché which acted as a complete non-conductor to the reader's emotion. From this poem I collected 'winging a thought,' 'a-thrill,' ''tis,' 'scarce,' 'the great White Ray,' 'things that matter.' Another poet put 'knew' and 'too' in such a position in a *vers libre* poem that they sounded as if they were meant to rhyme. Another seems to have sent a villanelle. But I object that I don't know what the 'starry stream' is, or believe in 'a song made from a sigh.' Another poet calls his verse, 'The Mirror of the Spirit' and uses 'thee' and 'thou' throughout—'beauteous' and 'majestic quiver' appear to have been expressions that I found fault with saying 'I think that perhaps you felt that your thoughts and form were becoming a little prosaic and hoped to increase the poetic effect by using a diction which we usually associate with poetry. I do not think this device is ever a success.' (The readers of Mrs. Wilkinson's *New Voices* will remember her remarks about what she calls the ‘ Hath-doth ’ school.)

—“ You ask for criticism of your poems. I think perhaps the best criticism is contained in your own title for them—you call them ‘ Bird Poems.’ That is to say that you do not seem even to be ambitious of being more than a writer of minor verse. The first one, ‘ The Blackcap,’ is pretty, but I don’t like —in the second and third lines of the first verse— ‘ clap ’ and ‘ blackcap ’ being so near together. It is all right visually, but try and say it aloud and you will notice the awkwardness— ”

A lady I accuse of not being careful about words and employing the phrase ‘ mystic hush.’

Another uses ‘ throb ’ as a transitive verb.

Another poet is not careful enough of sense in his sonnet, in that he brackets ‘‘dust and mold.’ ‘ Mold is damp and clinging and dust flies about.’ When the “ dust-and-mold ” further proceeds to “engulf in its strife,” the reader feels you have got tangled up in your meaning, or are writing on a purely verbal plane. I do not fancy the three last lines really mean anything. The reader sees what you mean, but you have not expressed it. I should imagine that you read rather too much Wordsworth and even perhaps Young’s “ Night Thoughts ” or Thompson’s “ Seasons.” ’

Another sonneteer apparently rhymed ‘ flock ’ and ‘ awoke,’ he then proceeded to ‘feel a rumbling’ and to ‘ hear a struggle.’ Afterwards somebody— the dawn, I think,—was ‘ clothed in beams of ruddy light,' but continued to throw 'a pale vagueness.' 'Haply' also occurred.

I have quantities of poems by children sent me. Fourteen seems a favourite age at which to aspire to publication. The chief fault of these poems is that they are either very stilted and read like verse essays by Dr. Johnson—the result of having been obliged to take a country walk,—or else they are about elves and birds and are conveyed in a horribly tinkling metre. These are apt to have such titles as 'The Song of the Hill-top Sprite.'

I never feel a great conviction that my letters of advice are much good—little squalid scraps of rule-of-thumb empiricism, that is what they amount to. However, they apparently give pleasure and encouragement. The only real advice that one can give to a poet is that he must try to read the right stuff and to try and acquire the right attitude of mind towards his work. Especially I should advise young poets not to despise theory, or to go off with the idea that rules will stop the fine flow of inspiration. To argue like this shows no psychological knowledge and very little commonsense, for the whole of human practice in acquiring skill, especially, of course, manual skill, is based on the fact that what you do consciously to-day, to-morrow and the next day, you will do in a week's time automatically. To practise your music, or service at tennis, or off-drive at cricket is really the process of teaching tricks to your subconsciousness. Just so you can get into the habit of writing skilfully. If you at first consciously seek certain merits and try to avoid certain faults, you will find yourself working automatically on a much higher level of skill,—you will find that you will have educated the afflatus. I do not mean to say that the young poet must write quantities of practice poems, I should think in most cases this would be as great as mistake as for an athlete to train by rushing as hard as possible every day up a very steep hill carrying a heavy load, both processes would be likely to strain the heart—both are in fact too arduous and disagreeable. But every poet, indeed every writer, goes about turning phrases to himself, just as every painter goes about making compositions out of what he sees. Here is the medium in which to practise.

Another thing in which the poet can help himself is in seeing to it that he has good conditions for his work. If possible he ought to be in constant contact with other poets, or at any rate with other artists of some sort. If this is really impossible (it seldom is), at least let him read a great deal, to counteract the suggestion which is then sure to be to some extent present in his environment, that 'all this is great nonsense.'

But perhaps the most difficult problem of all that many young poets have to face is the financial one. I think for most imaginative writers, especially when they are young, it is extremely bad absolutely to be obliged to write in order to pay for meat, bread and washing. Such a goad produces a sort of feverishness and self-consciousness that makes work a torture. For most writers it is far better to have a mechanical profession, even if such a profession gives him disagreeably little time for his real work. The more mechanical that profession is the better; —I mean that to be a schoolmaster or to keep a shop does not at all meet the case. It would be far better to be a tram-conductor. Agricultural labour, navvying and boiler-rivetting, of course, on the other hand, would be no good. A poet is not likely to do good work whose mind is drugged by the deadly physical fatigue which overcomes the amateur at such tasks.

And one more tip. Though a young writer must read a great deal, let him beware of poetic authors who have the sort of effect that Sir Thomas Browne has upon prose writers. Sir Thomas Browne's style is more catching than the plague; it is an extremely beautiful style, but it is almost always highly unsuitable for the business that the modern writer has in mind.

But I don't think that the young poet ought ever to be afraid of reading too much in general lest he should find that all the good songs have been sung. We live in the early time of a new phase and, unless the poet knows himself to be incurably imitative, it does not matter to him very much how often a thing has been said as long as it has not been said within the last fifteen years. For, if he has a modern mind, he will find that he approaches his subject so completely from a new angle that it will not matter in the least if he has tried to express the same things as some older poet. This is, of course, not only true of this age. It is obvious that it would not matter at all to Dryden that he and Gower had both written about Cressida; it would not have mattered to Dr. Johnson if Massinger had treated the subject of 'Irene,' it would only have been an obstacle to his writing his tragedy if Pope had done so.

'But,' says the poet, 'it is the moderns I fear. I don't want to cramp myself by knowing how Robert Nicholls has treated a theme of which I propose to write.' My advice to him is, however, to be ready to know the worst. If he has any contradictiousness in his nature the fact that Robert Nicholls has treated it in one way, will immediately suggest to him an alternate method.

Besides it is essential that he should read a great deal of modern poetry. Only, I think, by reading verse of their own epoch can writers or readers learn anything about the essence of poetry. As it is exemplified in the contemporary verse of any age, poetry shows stripped of a great deal of the adventitious glamour which surrounds the products of a different epoch. We are almost all of us in danger of liking obsolete words and poetic diction too much or too little. It is everything for the young person, and especially the young writer to have a chance of seeing the essential qualities of poetry without the slight muddle which this complication introduces.

PART IV

(FOR CRITICS)

CHAPTER XVII

THE FUNCTION OF CRITICISM

MR. Flint, in an amusing essay in one of the Poetry book-shop's Chapbooks, declared that the critic and the reviewer not only never are, but never can be of any use in the republic of letters. Critics are, he and Mr. Harold Monro hold, nothing but middlemen who snatch an unearned profit, both of money and applause, by coming officiously between consumer and producer. But of all critics he arraigns the reviewer especially. The reviewer, he says, with his summaries too often gives the reader the impression that to have perused his review is almost the same as to have read the book reviewed, while as a rule, except in the case of negligible literary productions, a summary gives a maimed and distorted view of the author's real achievement and a misleading impression of his views. It is almost bound, in any case, to be a version which, in the case of an argument, is a *résumé* with all the subtlety left out, and in the case of a work of art, is a skeleton with all the beauty gone. This is, he says, particularly true in the case of poetry.

'The only proper motive of the review is to call attention to something good and new. And this is exactly the motive which least often animates the re-

> viewer. That it should be so is not wholly the reviewer's fault. For reviewing is, unfortunately, a means of livelihood; though it is known to be one of the most corrupting, degrading, and badly-paid means of livelihood that a writing man can ply. The reviewers are merely the lowest wage-slaves in the modern literary system. Many intelligent men find themselves in this condition; it is part of the social organisation or disorganisation that writers who have honest work of their own to do find that this is the only work for which they can be paid. Consequently, it is hardly to be expected that the reviewer, unless he has become so depraved as to have no other function, should enjoy reviewing. From the point of view of any man with the slightest intellect or taste, there is not enough good verse to occupy a reviewer one week out of the year. There is not enough pernicious work worth attacking to occupy him another week. So that twenty-five twenty-sixths of the reviewer's time must be occupied with books that are perfectly colourless. And the dilemma is this: either a reviewer is a bad writer and bad critic, and he ought not to be allowed to intervene between books and the public; or he is a good writer and a good critic, and therefore ought not to be occupied in writing about inferior books.'

Reviewing, he goes on, is only valuable in so far as it is discreet advertisement: 'It cannot be too often insisted that the purpose—not of writing poetry, but of publishing it—should be primarily to give pleasure; and that the purpose for which we suppose reviewing was divinely intended was primarily to indicate such works as can give the best pleasure to the people who otherwise may fail to hear of their existence.'

Here Mr. Flint is beginning to perceive what is the true, if humble, function of the critic and of the reviewer. Hitherto, be it noticed, he has spoken entirely from the point of view of the 'producer,' never from that of the 'consumer.' But consider, for instance, the debt owed by the public to Mr. Edmund Gosse, that incomparable sleuth-hound. But for him, how many treasures would have been lost? We should have cause to be grateful to him, if only as the preserver and discoverer of the half-dozen first-rate stanzas that Toru Dutt had to give to the world. With the analytical critic Mr. Flint will have no truck at all; if the work criticised is a good work of art, he says the critic should just tell us shortly that this is his opinion; if it is bad, let him say so briefly. We can imagine Mr. Flint reducing the whole affair to a matter of plus and minus signs.

But certain objections will immediately present themselves in the reader's mind to Mr. Flint's line of argument. In the first place, he divides poetical output into good verse, pernicious verse, and colourless verse, and complains that the reviewer's time will be chiefly occupied with colourless verse. Here we have an instance of what I said before, *i.e.* that the difficulty about the school of criticism to which Mr. Flint, Mr. Elliot, Mr. Pound and Mr. Munro belong is that they do not envisage the common facts of life; they live in a world of their own. What are the facts? Not very much like Mr. Flint's picture of them. For the last two or three years, the entire output of published English verse has passed through my hands, and it is the most rough and ready analysis, the most bald inaccuracy that would divide the books which actually come under a critic purview into good, pernicious and colourless. Let us, for the sake of clarity, take the good books first, and let us take the word 'criticism' as meaning 'blame.' In the first place, directly we come to consider any actual book of verse—even if it be a long narrative poem like 'Right Royal' or 'Paris and Helen,' we find that it can hardly ever be treated as an entity. In all 'good books' we shall find a passage where the poet achieves what we will, for convenience, call absolute excellence, but he will not achieve it throughout the book. This fact, that the book does not always come up to the level of the best passages—or, if you prefer it, is always adorned by passages of outstanding merit—will be perceived by the person who is generally called the 'general reader,' but whom I should prefer to call 'the non-professional reader.' But he will apprehend the inferior parts rather as a sufferer from slight toothache perceives his discomfort; he realises that there is something wrong, but cannot locate his trouble as the malice of any particular tooth. When he goes to his dentist, the dentist probably says, 'Which tooth is it that is hurting you?' and he confesses that he does not know, and can only vaguely indicate its whereabouts. The dentist, as a man of science, who deals with nice concrete things like inflamed nerves, abscesses, or gumboils, is able to tell the enquirer exactly what is wrong, and, if he wants to, to put a little cross against the tooth on a chart. The non-professional reader of poetry is apt to appeal to the critic in the same sort of way, but now we are dealing with the world of ideas, a world in which the dentist's mark on a chart and Mr. Flint's plus and minus signs are seldom appropriate. But even in this comparatively nebulous region, practice and a certain faculty of selective attention, natural or acquired in the professional critic, will make him able to put his finger at least on the grosser errors. He will be able to point out, say, the long passage which, postponing the crisis of a narrative poem, has acted as a non-conductor to the reader's emotion and sent him away with a sense of puzzle and bafflement. He will 'show up' the borrowed or cliche-filled opening lines, which made it impossible for the reader to enjoy the remaining excellence of the sonnet. Or again, to resume our metaphor, the enquirer's discomfort may not have been from an aching tooth at all; it may not have been altogether the poet's fault that his reader was dissatisfied. Misunderstandings between poet and reader occur and can sometimes be remedied by a word of explanation. In every work of art the artist has probably more than once been obliged to choose between two alternative excellences—to steer between Scylla and Charybdis. He has wanted to express some very subtle idea, and there seemed no way of expressing it except by an oddity—some eccentricity of expression. The fact of the eccentricity will perhaps be the first thing to catch the non-professional reader's attention. He will very likely be upset by it and deprecate it so extremely that he may be unable to perceive the reason for its employment. If the poet's notion is explained to him in prose in a roundabout way, and it is pointed out that under the circumstances the oddity, though deprecated by the poet, was the only way of introducing the thought or the image, then he may become reconciled to it. A good many words or phrases have achieved general acceptance in some such way as this, and the language has thus been enriched by being made more capable of expressing some concept with sharpness and subtlety.

In fine, if in the 'good book' what has been explained away is a particular fault, its isolation and a frank admission of its existence will leave the reader freer to enjoy the excellence of the work. It may also have an effect upon the writer. We are not to treat the books we have under censure as the last products of their makers, a piece of criticism is often as helpful to an author, especially a young one, as it is to his reader. I remember when I was about seventeen I wrote a sort of historical pageant which was acted by amateurs and then published. It illustrated the history of British naval power. I liked it when it was done, but I could see that there was something wrong about it. I shall not easily forget my gratitude to one reviewer—I think of the *Westminster Gazette*—who put his finger on one of the blemishes that had puzzled me. I had not introduced a single sailor into any one of my five naval episodes! It can be believed that this had given a somewhat detached, not to say dessicated flavour to my production. But older and better writers than I have sometimes been puzzled exactly to locate the faults of their productions, even when these productions came distinctly under the category of 'good' works. For it is a commonplace that no work of a poet quite equals his original conception or completely bodies forth what he had to say. If then even good books may sometimes be helped to more appreciative readers or better successors by an exposition of their faults, how much may not be done with the books which Mr. Flint classes as colourless or pernicious. Here the critic is most needed in his capacity as gardener. He must shoo off readers whose taste might be corrupted by the futilities of the pernicious books; he must examine the weedy patches of the 'colourless' books in the hope of giving a chance to some genuine, if at the moment feeble poetic rootlet. All this is work which the critic can perform even in the most restricted view of his powers. Of his real function of praise, synthesis and explanation, I have as yet said nothing.

But all the same, Mr. Flint has some reason on his side. In a perfect world it may well be that there will be no need for the critic. Perfect reader and perfect poet may reach a perfect understanding. I for one shall mildly regret my office though I realise that in saying so I lay myself open to the accusation which Mr. Flint levels against the contented critic—that he has become so depraved as to have no other function. But in the world as it is, neither readers nor writers are perfect, though it makes a consideration of the functions of the critic easier if we assume that they are generally both sufficiently well-intentioned and honest. Their mutual incomprehension will give the critic work enough without considering the case of the malefactors.

What are the causes that make for misunderstanding? Let us take first the question of the progress, or to be more strictly neutral and not to confuse the issue by a statement that can in any way be held controversial, let us say the movement of the arts. Poetry is almost certain, from the nature of things, to move more quickly from phase to phase than the public for whom it is intended. The main preoccupation of poets is their work, and poetic movements are always, therefore, in the position of flying columns. They travel in three years through a space which it will take the general reader, who is encumbered with the baggage of many other interests—politics or poultry-keeping—ten to accomplish. It is the function of the critic to act as a sort of connecting file between the two parties.

Though the public may be slow, there is no question that poets are often precipitate. If, as I main tain, the function of the arts is to provide the best and subtlest kind of expression and communication between one human being and another, it is obviously a great loss if the poet writes in some sort of cipher which only the adept can understand. *Per contra* there is no doubt that the plain man will have to enlarge his vocabulary now and then if he is to get the full benefit of the poet's expositions. It is in this work that the critic can be of use.

There is, of course, a curious historical instance of the 'time lag' between the poet and his audience. In this instance—because it occurred at a time when the language was in a fluid state, the lag worked, paradoxically enough, the other way round. During the period of about fifty years which elapsed between Chaucer's death and the work of Barclay, Skelton and Surrey, the language in which Chaucer wrote had become so completely obsolete—final e's had been dropped, French pronunciations anglicised—that even the proper scansion of 'The Rhyme Royal' was lost, and in their rough, often unscanable work, the Tudor poets honestly believed themselves to be following exactly in the footsteps of their master Chaucer, whose work they couldn't make scan in the least. Such, however, was their 'Heart of Oak' loyalty to him, that they patiently copied what surely even to them must have seemed blemishes. There was here no connecting file between the poet and his audience. (Readers who desire to pursue this curious point will find it set out in Professor Berdan's 'Early Tudor Poetry, 1485—1547,' published in 1921.)

But even these expository functions, almost essential though they are, are subordinate to the critic's real function towards the poet. I have tried in a former chapter to prove partly on commonsense lines, partly in view of the theory of the arts as a subtle form of communication, that a poet needs a public almost as much as a public needs a poet. He needs to know that he has an audience. To shout the inmost secrets of your soul down a tunnel and not to be sure that the person at the other end is listening, or even that he has not gone away, is so depressing as to be an almost impossible task. Now all the people who read a poet's verse cannot write to the poet and tell him what they think about it. If we knew that the penalty for reading a book of verse was a long letter to its author, we should most of us give up reading poetry at all. But the public need not do that, for it has, or should have, a functionary at hand who can act as its spokesman—that functionary is the reviewer, who speaks from 'the receiving end' of the poem. He tells Mr. Bays that his verse is being read, he describes, or should describe, the reaction of a reader to the poem, and last, and most important of all, he praises. He does not necessarily eulogise, some kinds of blame can be a subtle and stimulating form of praise. A poet, say, has written two little volumes of verse into which he has put his whole heart, he has torn pieces out of his live flesh to put into the books. Then in a mood of reaction, or because he wants to make a little money, he perhaps contemptuously offers a third to the public—the leavings of the first two, patched-up stuff where the clay hopelessly outbulks the gold. If nobody sees the difference between the two first books and this third, the poet will probably become completely disheartened. Nobody has noticed! If he ever should do a good piece of work again and should it evoke praise from the critics, that praise will now be tainted and savourless to him because he knows that such commendation falls on the just and the unjust. In fact, we might almost say that he publishes his bad book hoping and praying that someone will notice the difference between it and its predecessors and will take the trouble of trouncing him. But whenever a good poet seems to be really trying his utmost, whenever he produces even a few lines that are obviously excellent, he ought to be praised for it. Praise is necessary to him, for the act of composition has after-effects like those that follow on any state of exhilaration; he has been in travail with his thought and, unlike the mother of a child, he is apt to look at the product of his pain, and wonder if it is good enough. And if it is good enough, if the fruit of his labour is a beautiful thing which we have enjoyed, the least we can do is to tell him that it *was* worth it, to cheer him up, to pat him on the back and to tell him of the pleasure that his striving with his material gave us. But why labour an elementary point? It is clear in every other field of human endeavour that, if we are decently humane, we shall get more out of our 'profitable servant.' Why should this be deemed to be less true in the case of the artist, who is the most sensitive of the servants of the community, the man who above all others will value the intangible gratifications of praise and prestige?

Chapter XVIII

THE VICES AND VIRTUES OF THE OLD CRITICS

If we are now inclined to hold that the functions of a critic of one of the arts are those which we endeavoured to outline in the last chapter, *i.e.* a sort of cross between that of a missionary and matrimonial agent, it becomes not uninteresting to consider how the critics of a past age regarded themselves.

Let us take as typical some of those who wrote most agreeably. We shall find that Dryden, Dr. Johnson and Peacock, for example, have one or two characteristics in common which differentiate them considerably from modern critics. In the first place—and here we must emphatically include Spenser—they wrote very much better for the most part. To say this is at once to praise and to blame, for in their work we are often conscious that they are not really offering us criticism at all, but have gone off and done a little piece of creative work on their own. A thousand times the better, of course, if a critical product be both a good intrinsic work of art and also a good piece of reasoning, analysis or appreciation. But the old critics are apt to sacrifice the purpose of their work for the sake of charming the reader, or rather in a fit of irresistible enthusiasm, they take part in the game which they should umpire. Again, Johnson, Dryden and Peacock take a great deal more 'as read' than the modern critic does. Their own position, that of art, and that of the reader, seem to them so obvious as not to need any particular exposition. Last of all—and this is to my mind their chiefest virtue—they all possess gusto. They love beauty, they love learning, they enjoy their tasks.

This love of his subject, combined with his captivating style and his exquisite freshness, makes Sidney's *Defence of Poesie* one of the most enchanting of books. In reading it we seem to have ecaped into a sort of Paradise. In the delicious atmosphere that he creates all need for the pedantries of comparison and analysis, the tedious weighing of poetry in the scales of aesthetic value, drop away from us. The spirit of lyric poetry seems to walk by us and infuse us with her delight. And all the time, though he never quite openly tells us what it is he knows, we are sure that this divine child has penetrated to a knowledge of the inner poetic truths. We feel, as we walk with Sidney down these flowering meadows, like the youth in the 'Romaunt of the Rose.' He, rising early on a sunny May morning and crossing through the fields and past the brooks, finds a high garden wall in front of him with its green door ajar, and suddenly enters into that fresh place of birds, flowers, fountains and of grass, where later, Love is to shoot at him, and where he finds the crimson rosebud.

Let me recall this divine treatise to the reader. He will perhaps forgive me if I quote rather at length from a book which he may have at hand on his shelves. If I merely give him chapter and verse he will not take it down I will wager, so if for the purposes of the contentions of this book I want him to know two or three passages which are contained in it, I must set down all of Sidney that he is to know. My purpose in dealing thus at length with a past critical age is to bring out two points.

First I want to show that many of the contentions as to the nature of poetry which I have tried to prove here are not invented either by me or by any other present-day critic. Look carefully at what I have quoted from Sidney's *Defense*, and you will see the germs of most of the modern aesthetic beliefs which I have attempted to state. The only new element is that we have endeavoured to make as much as possible of an old poetic faith, conscious and explicit. Sidney asserts. We have endeavoured to support similar assertions by argument.

Secondly, I want to exemplify what I believe, that is, that criticism is not as Mr. Flint tries to persuade us, necessarily dull to read nor 'degrading' to write.

Sidney's book opens with the praises of that band of poets who of old were the first 'that made pennes deliverers of their knowledge to posteritie.'

These were the poets who 'with their charming sweetness drew wild, untamed wits to an admiration of knowledge.'

> 'So as Amphion, was said to moove stones with his Poetry, to build Thebes, and Orpheus to be listned to by beasts, indeed stonie and beastly people.'

The philosophers of Greece, he goes on, for a long time concealed themselves under the mask of poets and sang their philosophy in verse, 'or rather they being poets, did exercise their delightful vaine in those points of highest knowledge.'

All others, such as actors and players, astronomers, geometricians, arithmeticians, grammarians, rhetoricians and logicians, natural and moral philosophers, are all men who only build upon the depth of nature, and 'without the works of nature they could not consist.'

> 'Only the Poet disdeining to be tied to any such subjection, lifted up with the vigor of his own invention, doth grow in effect into an other nature: in making things either better than nature bringeth foorth, or quite a new, formes such as never were in nature: as the Heroes, Demigods, Cyclops, Chymeras, Furies, and such like; so as he goeth hand in hand with nature, not enclosed within the narrow warrant of her gifts, but freely raunging within the Zodiack of his owne wit. Nature never set foorth the earth in so rich Tapistry as diverse Poets have done, neither with so pleasaunt rivers, fruitfull trees, sweete smelling flowers, not whatsoever els may make the too much loved earth more lovely: her world is brasen, the Poets only deliver a golden. But let those things alone and goe to man, for whom as the other things are, so it seemeth in him her uttermost cunning is imploied: and know whether she have brought foorth so true a lover as Theagenes, so

constant a friend as Pylades, so valiant a man as Orlando, so right a Prince as Xenophon's Cyrus, so excellent a man every way as Virgil's Aeneas.'

Sidney will have his poets defined and confined by no rules of rhyme or of metre.

'There have been most excellent poets that never versified: as Xenophon or Heliodorus in his sugared invention of that picture of love in Theagenes and Chariclea. It is not ryming and versing that maketh a Poet, (no more than a long gown maketh an Advocate, who though he pleaded in Armour, should be an Advocate and no souldier) but it is that faining notable images of vertues, vices, or what els, with that delightful teaching, which must be the right describing note to know a Poet by. Although indeed the Senate of Poets hath chosen verse as their fittest raiment: meaning as in matter, they passed all in all, so in maner, to go beyond them: not speaking table talke fashion, or like men in a dreame, words as they chanceably fall from the mouth, but peasing each sillable of eache word by just proportion, according to the dignitie of the subject.'

The end of all philosophy, of music, of mathematics and of astronomy is, he continues, 'but to draw us to as high a perfection as our degenerate selves might well be capable of.'

The end of all earthly learning is virtuous action, those 'whose skill most serves to bring forth that have a just title to be Princes over all the rest.' Are we to give this title to the poet or to the man of ethics? Forth steps, says Sidney, the moral philosopher,

'whom me thinkes I see comming towards me, with a sullain gravitie, as though they could not abide vice by day-light, rudely cloathed, for to witnesse outwardly

> their contempt of outward things, with bookes in their hands against glorie, whereto they set their names: sophistically speaking against subtilitie, and angry with any man in whom they see the foule fault of anger. One that hath no other guide but a phylosopher shall wade in him till he be olde, before he shall finde sufficient cause to be honest. For his knowledge standeth so upon the abstract and generall, that happie is that man who may understand him, and more happie, that can apply what he dothe understand. On the other side, the Historian wanting the precept, is so tied, not to what should be, but to what is, to the particular truth of things, and not to the general reason of things, that his example draweth no necessarie consequence, and therefore a lesse fruitfull doctrine. Now doth the peerlesse Poet performe both, for whatsoever the Philosopher saith should be done, he gives a perfect picture of it by some one, by whom he presupposeth it was done, so as he coupleth the general notion with the particular example. . . . For as in outward things to a man that had never seene an Elephant, or a Rinoceros, who should tell him most exquisitely all their shape, cullour, bignesse, & particuler marks, or of a gorgious pallace an Architecture, who declaring the full beawties, might well make the hearer able to repeat as it were by roat, all he had heard, yet should never satisfie his inward conceit, with being witnesse to it selfe of a true lively knowledge.'

For there are many infallible grounds of wisdom which

> 'lie darke before the imaginative and judging power, if they be not illuminated or figure forth by the speaking picture of Poesie. . . . Certainly even our Saviour Christ could as well have given the morall common places of uncharitablenesse and humblenesse, as the divine narration of Dives & Lazarus, or of disobedience & mercy, as that heavenly discourse of the lost childe and the gracious Father, but that his through searching wisedome, knew the estate of Dives burning in hell, &

> of Lazarus in Abraham's bosome, would more constantly as it were, inhabit both the memorie and judgement. Truly, for my selfe (me seemes) I see before mine eyes, the lost childs disdainful prodigalitie, turned to envy a Swines dinner: which by the learned Divines are thought not Historical acts, but instructing Parables . . . But the Poet is the food for the tendrest stomacks, the Poet is indeed, the right populer Philosopher.'

We shall not find such insight till we come to the epoch of Matthew Arnold, and nowhere else in the world, I think, shall we find the case for poetry stated with such magical beauty.

If Sidney gave to poets in general their proper place in the scheme of things, Johnson admirably fulfilled the critic's other task of putting a particular writer and his public *en rapport*. He made many mistakes. A man so didactic, so fond of a positive assertion could not fail to do that. For instance, he levelled against Gray's 'Ruin seize thee, ruthless king'—I forget in what words—the sort of accusation that many critics now apply to the work of poets like the Sitwells. He declared that the poem being merely odd, though very popular at the moment, could obviously not possibly live. There was a great deal of Shakespeare that Johnson could not understand, but to the merits that he did perceive, even when they were not merits that he personally valued very much, he was scrupulously fair. His sense of justice was always indeed one of the outstanding features of his dealings with the poets whom he criticised. A perfect example, of course, at once of his humour and of his candour is found in

The Lives of the Poets in his phrase about the minor poet whose work he felt he ought to like better: 'I had rather praise him than read him.' What reviewer has not echoed that saying! Once brief Dr. Johnson for a poet, and he would generally search out every possible merit in him.

His most amusing criticisms are generally allowed to be contained in the various things that he wrote about Shakespeare, notably *The Proposals for Printing the Dramatic Works of William Shakespeare*, and the Preface to this edition, when executed. In 1756, when the book was published, Shakespeare still required a great deal of 'explaining away' and suffered then, as now, alike from absurd adulation and from stupid misunderstanding. The intellectual bloods of the day reacted as surely to the adulation then current as did Mr. Shaw or as do still a dozen young people of light and leading to the present atmosphere of Stratford-on-Avon. Dr. Johnson opens his remarks with a right and left at both unthinking admirers and mechanical disparagers:

> 'That praises are without reason lavished on the dead, and that the honours due only to excellence are paid to antiquity, is a complaint likely to be always continued by those, who, being able to add nothing to truth, hope for eminence from the heresies of paradox.'

Johnson was always careful to point out that Shakespeare must not be judged by the standard of modern poets, because

> 'his allusions are so often undiscovered, and many beauties, both of pleasantry and greatness, are lost with

the objects to which they were united, as the figures vanish when the canvass has decayed.'

How are we, he asks, to rank time tests? In the passage in which he states his views we have one of the best examples of the peculiarly vigorous powers of Dr. Johnson's mind, and perhaps of its curious limitations.

'What mankind have long possessed they have often examined and compared; and if they persist to value the possession, it is because frequent comparisons have confirmed opinion in its favour. As among the works of nature no man can properly call a river deep, or a mountain high, without the knowledge of many mountains, and many rivers; so, in the productions of genius, nothing can be styled excellent till it has been compared with other works of the same kind. Demonstration immediately displays its power, and has nothing to hope or fear from the flux of years; but works tentative and experimental must be estimated by their proportion to the general and collective ability of man, as it is discovered in a long succession of endeavours. Of the first building that was raised, it might be with certainty determined that it was round or square; but whether it was spacious or lofty must have been referred to time. The *Pythagorean* scale of numbers was at once discovered to be perfect; but the poems of *Homer* we yet know not to transcend the common limits of human intelligence, but by remarking, that nation after nation, and century after century, has been able to do little more than transpose his incidents, new-name his characters, and paraphrase his sentiments.

'The reverence due to writings that have long subsisted arises therefore not from any credulous confidence in the superiour wisdom of past ages, or gloomy persuasion of the degeneracy of mankind, but is the consequence of acknowledged and indubitable positions, that what has been longest known has been most considered, and what is most considered is best understood.'

Dr. Johnson not only knew how to praise, but he knew how to frame his eulogies so that we should be eager to read them.

'It was said of *Euripides*, that every verse was a precept; and it may be said of *Shakespeare*, that from his works may be collected a system of civil and economical prudence. Yet his real power is not shown in the splendour of particular passages, but by the progress of his fable, and the tenor of his dialogue; and he that tries to recommend him by select quotations, will succeed like the pedant in *Hierocles*, who, when he offered his house for sale, carried a brick in his pocket as a specimen. . . .

'The theatre, when it is under any other direction, is peopled by such characters as were never seen, conversing in a language which was never heard, upon topicks which will never arise in the commerce of mankind.

'Upon every other stage the universal agent is love, by whose power all good and evil is distributed, and every action quickened or retarded. To bring a lover, a lady, and a rival into the fable; to entangle them in contradictory obligations, perplex them with oppositions of interest, and harass them with violence of desires inconsistent with each other; to make them meet in rapture, and part in agony; to fill their mouths with hyperbolical joy and outrageous sorrow; to distress them as nothing human ever was distressed; to deliver them as nothing human ever was delivered; is the business of a modern dramatist. For this, probability is violated, life is misrepresented, and language is depraved. . . .

'Other dramatists can only gain attention by hyperbolical or aggravated characters, by fabulous and unexampled excellence or depravity, as the writers of barbarous romances invigorated the reader by a giant and a dwarf; and he that should form his expectations of human affairs from the play, or from the tale, would be equally deceived. *Shakespeare* has no heroes; his scenes are occupied only by men, who act and speak as the reader thinks that he should himself have spoken or acted on the same occasion; even where the agency is supernatural, the dialogue is level with life. . . . It may be said that he has not only shown human nature as it acts in real exigencies, but as it would be found in trials to which it cannot be exposed.'

Shakespeare's drama 'is the mirror of life.' There we may read 'human sentiments in human language,' witness 'scenes from which a hermit may estimate the transactions of the world, and a confessor predict the progress of the passions.'

Dennis and Rymer think his Romans not sufficiently Roman; and Voltaire censures his kings as not completely royal. A senator, say they, should not be made to play the buffoon, and it is indecent to represent the Danish usurper as a drunkard.

'Shakespeare's story requires *Romans* or Kings, but he thinks only on men. He knew that *Rome*, like every other city, had men of all dispositions; and wanting a buffoon, he went into the senate-house for that which the senate-house would certainly have afforded him. He was inclined to show an usurper and a murderer not only odious, but despicable; he therefore added drunkenness to his other qualities, knowing that kings love wine like other men, and that wine exerts its natural power upon kings. These are the petty cavils of petty minds; a poet overlooks the casual distinction of country and condition.'

Here and there, however, Johnson dates himself and shows the narrow grooves in which contemporary morals had contrived to make even his vigorous mind run. He is entirely persuaded, for instance, that it is the duty of a poet to be didactic, to play the 'hortatory policeman.' He takes this as basic and axiomatic, and arraigns Shakespeare because

> 'he sacrifices virtue to convenience and is so much more careful to please than to instruct, that he seems to write without any moral purpose. From his writings indeed a system of social duty may be selected, for he that thinks reasonably must think morally; but his precepts and axioms drop casually from him; he makes no just distribution of good or evil, nor is always careful to show in the virtuous a disapprobation of the wicked; he carries his persons indifferently through right and wrong, and at the close dismisses them without further care, and leaves their examples to operate by chance. This fault the barbarity of his age cannot extenuate; for it is always a writer's duty to make the world better, and justice is a virtue independent of time or place.'

It is in the section devoted to blaming Shakespeare that we shall find the famous passage on quibbles:

> 'A quibble is to *Shakespeare* what luminous vapours are to the traveller; he follows it at all adventures; it is sure to lead him out of his way, and sure to engulf him in the mire. It has some malignant power over his mind, and its fascinations are irresistible. Whatever be the dignity or profundity of his disquisition, whether he be enlarging knowledge or exalting affection, whether he be amusing attention with incidents, or enchaining it in suspense, let but a quibble spring up before him, and he leaves his work unfinished. A quibble is the golden apple for which he will always turn aside from his career, or stoop from his elevation. A quibble, poor and barren as it is, gave him such delight, that he was content to purchase it, by the sacrifice of reason, propriety, and truth. A quibble was to him the fatal *Cleopatra* for which he lost the world, and was content to lose it.'

But this vigorous attack is followed by as warm a defence of Shakespeare's neglect of unities, especially of the unity of place. In this Johnson completely pulverises the wretched critics, who, he says, have hitherto exulted 'over the miseries of an irregular poet.' Dr. Johnson is ready to assure them that they are assuming, 'as an unquestionable principle, a position, which, while their breath is forming it into words, their understanding pronounces to be false.' The spectator of drama is not deluded, he does not believe 'that his walk to the theatre has been a voyage to Egypt,' or if he does (Johnson is ready with the butt end of his pistol), 'surely he that imagines this may imagine more.'

> 'Delusion has no certain limitations; if the spectator can be once persuaded that his old acquaintances are *Alexander* and *Cæsar*, that a room illuminated with candles is the plain of *Pharsalia*, or the bank of *Granicus*, he is in a state of elevation above the reach of reason, or of truth, and from the heights of empyrean poetry may despise the circumscriptions of terrestrial nature.'

The truth is, of course, 'that the spectators are always in their senses,' and if it be asked how the drama moves if it is not credited, the answer is that 'it is credited with all the credit due to a drama.' We believe in what we read in much the same way, and 'are agitated in reading *Henry the Fifth*. Yet no man takes his book for the field of *Agincourt*.'

But when Dr. Johnson goes on to speak of imitations, he wanders far from the truth after that will-o'-the-wisp, and supposes that the arts please because they bring realities to the mind.

There are, I think, not many more elements to be found in Johnson's literary criticism.

He wrote amusingly, he possessed immense volumes of commonsense which he discharged upon the public with unexampled vigour. But of Meredith's 'fine shades and nice feelings' he knew hardly anything, and so was always a better critic of the dramatic or narrative elements of literature than of the poetic.

When we turn from him to Peacock, or rather to that side of Peacock which the malign creature chose to display for the discomfiture of poor Shelley in his 'Four Ages of Poetry,' we shall find somewhat similar powers and similar limitations. The instruments—bludgeons both—are alike, though they are wielded to such different ends.

Peacock's 'Four Ages of Poetry' is, perhaps, the wittiest thing that that very witty writer ever wrote, and is the only piece of criticism which, for hilarious verve and the power to make the reader chuckle, can compare with Dr. Johnson's work. Much of it is very like 'Candide' in tone. That Shelley should have taken the attack as being a serious one, or as in the least representing the writer's opinion, is but one more proof of Shelley's inordinate ethical preoccupations and his unconquerable seriousness.

The four ages of poetry are, says Peacock, the ages of iron, of gold, of silver, and lastly of brass. In the iron age 'rude bards celebrate in rough numbers the exploits of ruder chiefs.' This, he goes on, 'is the age of society, when the maxim, To keep what we have and to catch when we can, is not yet disguised under names of justice and the forms of law.' This is the age when there are only three trades flourishing, 'those of king, thief and beggar: the beggar being for the most part a king deject and the thief a king expectant.' In such society every man not only desires to engross to himself as much power and property as possible, but he is affected by a longing for publicity. That is:

> 'The no less natural desire of making known to as many people as possible the extent to which he has been a winner in this universal game. The successful warrior becomes a chief; the successful chief becomes a king; his next want is an organ to disseminate the fame of his achievements and the extent of his possessions; and this organ he finds in a bard, who is always ready to celebrate the strength of his arm, being first duly inspired by that of his liquor.' The bard will 'tell us how many battles such an one has fought, how many helmets he has cleft, how many breastplates he has pierced, how many widows he has made, how much land he has appropriated, how many houses he has demolished for other people, what a large one he has built for himself, how much gold he has stowed away in it, and how liberally and plentifully he pays, feeds, and intoxicates the divine and immortal bards, the sons of Jupiter, but for whose everlasting songs the names of heroes would perish.'

He goes on to describe the process by which the golden age is reached. Though the object of the bards be nothing more than to secure a share of the spoil, they achieve their ends by different means; they are observing and thinking while others are robbing and fighting. They are not only historians, but theologians, moralists and legislators, and very soon gain the reputation of

> 'building cities with a song and leading brutes with a symphony,—which are only metaphors for the faculty of leading multitudes by the nose.'

It is not until we come to the age of silver, the age of recasting and of giving an exquisite polish to the poetry of the age of gold, the age of which Virgil is the most obvious and striking example, that we can pierce the perfect armour of Peacock's raillery, and catch him out in a sentiment at once genuine and absurd. He seems to agree with Macaulay, who said, 'We think that as civilisation advances, poetry almost necessarily declines.' As the light of reason grows clearer, says Peacock, poetry, the language of passion and feeling, approaches its extinction.

> 'Pure reason and dispassionate truth would be perfectly ridiculous in verse, as we may judge by versifying one of Euclid's demonstrations. This will be found true of all dispassionate reasoning whatever, and all reasoning that requires comprehensive views and enlarged combinations. It is only the more tangible points of morality, those which command assent at once, those which have a mirror in every mind, and in which the severity of reason is warmed and rendered palatable by being mixed up with feeling and imagination, that are applicable even to what is called moral poetry: and as the sciences of morals and of mind advance towards perfection, as they become more enlarged and comprehensive in their views, as reason gains the ascendancy in them over imaginations and feeling, poetry can no longer accompany them in their progress, but drops into the background, and leaves them to advance alone.'

We in this age are inclined instead to agree with Renan who, half serious, half whimsical, said that as he grew older he more and more inclined to the belief that many of the most profound truths were so subtle as to be incapable of being conveyed from one mind to another, except by such a vehicle as opera, a vehicle which brought all our sources of apprehension—our senses—into play. But Peacock is not at home among fundamentals. If we want to enjoy his full powers we must seek him in the top, in the sparkling, even the frothy regions of his subject. *Apropos* of the dramatic unities, he resumes his best Voltairian vein :

> 'Shakespeare and his contemporaries used time and locality merely because they could not do without them, because every action must have its when and where : but they made no scruple of deposing a Roman Emperor by an Italian Count and sending him off in the disguise of a French pilgrim to be shot with a blunderbuss by an English archer.'

But perhaps the most fascinating passage in the whole essay is the following tiny satiric picture of the Lake poets. These men, Peacock says, have argued thus :

> 'All that is artificial is anti-poetical. Society is artificial, therefore we will live out of society. The mountains are natural, therefore we will live in the mountains. There we shall be shining models of purity and virtue, passing the whole day in the innocent and amiable occupation of going up and down hill, receiving poetical impressions, and communicating them in immortal verse to admiring generations.'

Peacock affirms that he burns with impatience at

the sight of poets, all of whom, more or less, as science and philosophy advance, still 'wallow in the rubbish of departed ignorance, raking up the ashes of dead savages to find gewgaws and rattles for the grown babies of the age.'

Poor Shelley writhed under all this like a lost soul under the sly, red-hot prods of a small, malicious devil. But he could think of adequate answers to none of the impish jibes, and his 'Defence of Poetry' is a document to bring despair to the heart of the logically-minded. He commits all the crimes. He never defines, he uses the same word in two or three different senses, builds toppling pyramids of argument on foundations of gratuitous assumption, and, emerging giddy from the mazes of a circular argument, takes refuge in a page or two of unsupported *ex cathedra* statement. But with all its absurdities and faults there is something splendid about Shelley's 'Defence.' We feel the warmth and light of the authentic poetic fire.

He fully realises Renan's argument, but has, as usual, given no very clear utterance to it or to what he wants to say, particularly about metre, and has mixed it up with another point, *i.e.* the value of translations.

> 'The language of poets has ever affected a certain uniform and harmonious recurrence of sound, without which it were not poetry, and which is scarcely less indispensable to the communication of its influence than the words themselves, without reference to that peculiar order. Hence the vanity of translation: it were as wise to cast a violet into a crucible that you might discover

> the formal principle of its colour and odour, as seek to transfuse from one language into another the creations of a poet.'

He tries again. The following beautiful passage is the result:

> 'Poetry is ever accompanied with pleasure; all spirits upon which it falls open themselves to receive the wisdom which is mingled with its delight. In the infancy of the world, neither poets themselves nor their auditors are fully aware of the excellence of poetry: for it acts in a divine and unapprehended manner, beyond and above consciousness.'

Poets are looked for in ages of change and reform.

> 'We live among such philosophers and poets as surpass beyond comparison any who have appeared since the last national struggle for civil and religious liberty. The most unfailing herald, companion, and follower of the awakening of a great people to work a beneficial change in opinion and institution, is poetry. At such periods there is an accumulation of the power of communicating and receiving intense and impassioned conceptions respecting man and nature. The persons in whom this power resides may often, as far as regards many portions of their nature, have little apparent correspondence with that spirit of good of which they are the ministers.'
>
> 'Poets are the hierophants of an unapprehended inspiration; the mirrors of the gigantic shadows which futurity casts upon the present: the words which express what they understand not: the trumpets which sing to battle and feel not what they inspire: the influence which is moved not, but moves. Poets are the unacknowledged legislators of the world.'

Umpire, you have put off the white coat of neutrality and are trying your hand at the game! This is not criticism, this is poetry.

In the same volume of the Percy Reprints as 'The Four Ages of Poetry' and Shelley's Defence, Mr. Brett Smith has bound up Browning's Essay on Shelley, an essay unfortunately written, like Shelley's, in a rather lofty poétic-prose style. In spite of this unpromising medium, Browning has nevertheless been able to imprison in the essay some of his wonderful gift for psychology. Buried under the verbiage are some extremely interesting observations on the difference between objective and subjective poets. In speaking of Shelley, he generalises and speaks of the subjective poet in general:

> 'He is rather a seer, accordingly, than a fashioner, and what he produces will be less a work than an effluence. That effluence cannot be easily considered in abstraction from his personality,—being indeed the very radiance and aroma of his personality, projected from it but not separated.'

If we desire to understand his poetry, we must know something of the subjective poet's character:

> 'Both for love's and for understanding's sake we desire to know him, and as readers of his poetry we must be readers of his biography also.'

Very remarkable seems to me the passage which I like to take as prophetic,—a statement of the relative position of the Victorian and the modern poet:

> 'There is a time when the general eye has, so to speak, absorbed its fill of the phenomena around it, whether spiritual or material, and desires rather to learn the exacter significance of what it possesses, than to receive any augmentation of what is possessed.'

And in this passage we see the beginnings of the new spirit, a spirit which we find full-fledged in Matthew Arnold, a writer who but for the facts of chronology, I should certainly have included in the next chapter, and have considered with the new critics. In turning the pages of Matthew Arnold's critical essays, we find that we are in touch with a man with a modern outlook. There are differences between his writings and the writings of Mr. Heuffer and Mr. Flint—we cannot see either of these writers turning the famous passage whose refrain is 'Wragg is in custody.' But if I may allow myself for once to use what I have throughout this book studiously tried to avoid—the jargon of psycho-analysis—Matthew Arnold for the first time gives us the peculiar sort of introvertism that we get in modern writers. In the midst of the whirlwind of Victorian activity, he pleads for reflection, for a disinterested mode of looking at life and facts. Let us, he says, return to the serener life of the mind.

> 'Let us think of quietly enlarging our stock of true and fresh ideas, and not, as soon as we get an idea or half an idea, be running out with it into the street, and trying to make it rule there.'

It is the detachment which he expresses here which enables him to see the world of literature, not as consisting of 'English bards and Scotch reviewers' —that is, of two opposing camps of creative and critical minds, but as a body of people attempting by various but still somewhat similar methods to attain ends in the world of ideas. And in this larger vision he is easily able to pass from the critic to the creative writer and back again and apply the same general principle to them both.

> 'Judging is often spoken of as the critic's one business; and so in some sense it is; but the judgment which almost insensibly forms itself in a fair and clear mind, along with fresh knowledge, is the valuable one; and thus knowledge, and ever fresh knowledge, must be the critic's great concern for himself; and it is by communicating fresh knowledge, and letting his own judgment pass along with it—but insensibly, and in the second place, not the first, as a sort of companion and clue, not as an abstract lawgiver—that he will generally do most good to his readers.'

If, he goes on, the reader is disappointed because he does not speak directly of the critics and of the criticisms of the current English literature of the day, he is sorry,

> 'but I am bound by my own definition of criticism: *a disinterested endeavour to learn and propagate the best that is known and thought in the world.*'

He goes on to suggest that every critic of current English literature ought to try and possess one great literature besides his own, and the more unlike his own, the better.

> 'Europe must be regarded as being, for intellectual and spiritual purposes, one great confederation, bound to a joint action and working to a common result; and members must have, for their proper outfit, a knowledge of Greek, Roman, and Eastern antiquity, and of one another. That modern nation will, in the intellectual and spiritual sphere, make most progress, which most thoroughly carries out this programme.'

Perhaps some of us at this date would prefer to substitute for the critic's knowledge of antiquity, nay, even for his knowledge of another European literature, a knowledge of some aspects of those new facts about the human mind which psychology and metaphysics have recently made plain. Of course, the critic cannot know too much, and perhaps it is a personal idiosyncracy which makes me believe that a knowledge of, or at least an interest in, the facts which seem to underlie the apprehension and creation of literature, are likely to be of more value to the critic than a knowledge of another great literature, *i.e.* of a still larger number of instances of the phenomena of poetry.

It seems to me too that in working partly on psychological and metaphysical lines, not only has the critic the best chance of understanding the particular literature which he is studying, but he will perform another function, that of increasing the bonds which unite literature and life. For literature, and especially poetry, may be likened to the earth giant who fought with Hercules. He, the reader will remember, renewed his strength every time that Hercules' knock-down blow brought him into contact with the life-giving earth. When Hercules hit upon the device of detaching him from this revivifying contact with reality, his vigour withered away.

CHAPTER XIX

THE VICES AND VIRTUES OF THE NEW CRITICS.

SUPPOSE a new critic and an old were to be asked to deliver a lecture upon the Pictorial Arts in Verse. The old critic would begin by collecting all the instances he could think of—'Pope, Now! How did the passage run?'

> 'Come then the colours and the ground prepare!
> Dip in the rainbow, trick her off in air.'

and then:

> 'Beauty frail flower that every season fears
> Lives in thy canvas for a thousand years.'

Then Browning's 'Tobias and the Angel.' He would search the Chaucerians—all those 'Temples of Fame.' There was so much about architecture and sculpture, surely he could dig out something about painting too. Browning again, Fra Lippo Lippi and Raphael; then Wordsworth's 'The Light that never was on Sea or Land,' then various passages from 'Hero and Leander.' The modern critic, though he might very likely end by choosing out the same examples, would set to work quite differently. He would begin by trying to think out an abstract theory. How can the peculiar qualities of a thing which paint gives us—its degree of luminosity or the interaction of its curves, be treated in poetry? Apart from direct reference to painting, what poems are written from the painting point of view, with the visual qualities of the material objects uppermost? Would it be absurd to say that a poem about a picture will be at one removed from the natural object because it is a copy of a copy? A picture is *ding an sich*, an object just as a flower is, and indeed, in that it is to some extent a pre-digested object, it may be arguable that it is a better subject for a poet than a crude natural object. And so on. I am not concerned to pit these two methods against one another. I know, of course, to which extreme I incline, but I can see the dangers of both. The older critics, especially those of the era through which we have just passed, critics who wrote later than any of those whose views I have tried to set forth in the last chapter, were apt to become very much too concrete. They got interested in phenomena and in collecting more and more examples of phenomena, and often lost sight of the causes for which they studied. On the other hand, the analytical critic is apt to become too detached. It is, alas, so fatally easy to construct a self-supporting aesthetic theory which turns out to bear no relation whatever to the facts.

Mr. Squire, of course, began as an analytical critic, but his vivid interest in technique, his learning, and an admirable faculty for parody prevented his floating off too much into the vague. His later work shows him getting more and more to resemble writers of the older school. I personally share the view of a good many of his readers and see the change with regret, but on the other hand he used the modern method better—I do not want to call it the analytical method, for that unduly narrows my meaning—and carried analysis further than most of his contemporaries, and it may be that he has good reason for the gradual change in his attitude. One great blessing attends Mr. Squire. He writes amusingly. His remarkable gift for parody is, of course, a great asset here, enabling him, for example, to adorn and illustrate his remarks with mock examples. How will Prohibition affect the poet? Mr. Squire sees him struggling with a convivial song.

> 'Come, chemist, fill the silver box
> With morphia or with ether.'

He has further the valuable knack of conveying criticism without condemnation, as witness the following remarks about Mr. Drinkwater's 'Abraham Lincoln':

> 'I saw—at least I thought I saw—all sorts of defects in characterisation, interpretation, machinery; from the absence of that humour which always clung about the hero to the fact that the whole seven scenes took place indoors; from the melodrama of Mr. Hook to the unconvincing and overdone pathos of the condemned sentry, who was so handsome, so brave, spoke such perfect English, and had committed his offence under such extremely palliating circumstances that it was unbelievable that anyone can have meant to execute him. But the fact remains that my eyes and ears were glued to the actors throughout; that in places I was profoundly moved;

that I was as sorry when Lincoln was shot as I should have been had I been present at the event; and that I went away saying that not even the ban on smoking would keep me away from the theatre if there were many plays which appealed as this one had done to both my intelligence and my emotion. There is no poetry about Mr. Drinkwater's verse choruses, but there is a good deal in his prose-play.

'He partially escapes, in fact, the radical defects of the modern theatre. There is an immense amount of interest in the theatre. Books are written about its possibilities; societies are founded to explore and exploit them; everyone hopes that the theatre will in our time be as good as it was in the days of Shakespeare and Aeschylus; and thousands of persons with intellects write for the stage. But it is commonly overlooked that Shakespeare and his contemporaries, like Aeschylus and his contemporaries, were poets.'

I think a certain quality of tolerance, fairmindedness and kind-heartedness, combined with a searching faculty for stripping away clap-trap, are the qualities that have given Mr. Squire his unique position. He reigns a sort of king in Literary London, because he knows how to be both kind and severe to young writers. He is willing to take infinite trouble over work submitted to him and will labour with the author to improve and amend. Almost every young author who comes into contact with Mr. Squire feels first, that he must put his best foot foremost, and secondly that Mr. Squire still has the elasticity to give him appreciation.

Mr. Harold Munro has all the qualities of head that go to make a critic, but to my mind few of the qualities of heart. His 'Contemporary Poets' is practically a bitter attack upon the two or three dozen poets whose work he criticises. The reader closes the book with the impression that Miss Charlotte Mew is the only modern poet worth reading, an impression grotesque enough for him to be sure that this was not what Mr. Monro intended. What has happened apparently is that Mr. Monro has taken a dislike to poetry and wishes that people would stop writing it. As for the Founder of the Poetry Bookshop's indictment of the modern poetical coterie, it is as savage as it is amusing.

> 'It is related of one of our younger poets that he declared he would not publish a First Book until he knew sixteen critics personally, and had dined with each. . . . Verse-writing in the year 1920 is a professional occupation.'

Young men and women, he goes on, enjoy the practice of making rhymes, putting down their feelings in loose sentences which they call 'free verse.' Newspapers and magazines have a large demand for such work, but many as are the niches, the competition is great, and so the young poet's eye must ever be trained on the main chance. His first book will be a great event. It does not matter whether people read him or not, but at least twenty thousand people must talk about him.

Then, as soon as he gets to know a few people, he must talk to them of the Great Ones whom he does not know, 'for present acquaintance must be the stepping-stones to future ones':—

> 'He must learn how to joke cynically about the Great, and, if obliged to admit that he has not actually met Mr. H., Mr. N., or Sir S. G., must be able to imply

> skilfully that he will probably be dining with each of them next week. All this time, however, he must not cease to "write poetry."'

He must attach himself to some group which will quickly teach him to talk cleverly about modern painting, and books which he has not read; also it will publish a periodical or anthology in which his poems will be printed. His position must, in fact, be made before the verses which might warrant it have been written . . . . And so on in a heartfelt satiric vein. However, we are a little cheered when we read at the end of the book that Mr. Monro considers that 'verse is undoubtedly inferior to prose as a medium, but it is easier to write.' We begin to see daylight.

If he feels like this about poets, what will he have to say about fellow critics and reviewers? We feel that it is only too likely that he is going to agree with Mr. Flint, whose denunciation of my tribe I quoted tremblingly in the chapter before last:

> 'As for the professional critics, is it, I wonder, a revelation to anybody that in the majority of editorial offices preference is given to books whose publishers are advertisers in the paper?'

Mr. Harold Monro must keep uncommonly bad journalistic company. *The Spectator*, whose patient drudge I confess myself, is surely not in the position of lonely virtue that Mr. Monro's words would imply? He speaks again of 'tired critics, sometimes too hungry to object to writing what they are told,' of insipid critics who have 'two or three hundred *cliché* phrases at their command.' Every time a 'good' author publishes a book,

> 'a trained person has merely to jot down a series of the conventional phrases : "sustained inspiration," "finished craftsmanship," "essential quality of high poetry," "splendid and virile," "amongst the finest achievements of our age," "sounds depths only possible to a master," "never been surpassed," "noble," "notable," "felicitous"—we all know them so well that we do not trouble to pay the slightest attention to them."

These opinions show clearly that a good many of Mr. Monro's generalisations are due to the exaggeration of exasperation. I also examine 'a very large proportion of current books of poetry.' The chief difficulty of the honest critic is to keep his critical head above water and not to be submerged, or rather rolled out perfectly flat by the weight of books which pour on top of him. That is surely the chief, the simple reason for the many failures and ineptitudes of current reviewing. The critic may have to examine sixty or seventy poems in a morning, and by the time he has done thirty it requires a considerable exercise of self-discipline and concentration to keep the critical standard flying, not to condemn a good piece of work because it contains one or two atrocious lines, not to approve a competent poem which suffers only from the disability of having no reason for existing at all. As Mr. Monro himself says, the honest reviewer is kept up to his task by the one thought above all others :—

> 'Perhaps, high up on some shelf, neglected by the reviewers and by myself (a patient searcher), stands that

> ominous volume, a *Paradise Lost*, or *Songs of Innocence*, or *Prometheus Unbound* of this age, accumulating dust.'

That is the carrot.

The total impression of the book is one of hostility. Mr. Monro holds it a scandal and shame that there are so many bad poets and so many bad reviewers. Surely his attitude should be one of thankfulness that there are a very few good poets and a very few good reviewers. Poetasters and puffers are not a unique product of this age or of this country. It is significant that Mr. Monro never praises a poet for being readable, seemingly because he dislikes reading poetry. But we assure him that there are a great many people—the present writer included—who do like reading poetry, and therefore, notwithstanding any holes that can be justly picked in them, are extremely grateful for such poems as 'Daffodil Fields,' 'The Queen of China,' and 'The Moon.' Why not think of poetry as like cheese or apples, as being something necessary, instead of adopting the attitude of the man who has given five shillings for a cigar? However, the book is tonic to the system as well as bitter to the tongue. It will be splendid reading for a great many of the poets mentioned in it.

Mr. Monro knows what poetry ought to be made of, as witness the following passage:—

> 'Accurate observation, close inquiry, a respect for detail; selection, condensation, rejection of the unnecessary; choice of image, phrase or rhythm; aesthetic honesty, literary candour, local truth, psychological accuracy; prudent management of rhyme, economy of

epithet, love of the true substantive, pleasure in the right verb; imaginative curiosity, the joy of new philosophic discovery, the adventure of metaphysical speculation, the humility or courageous ardour of religious doubt, and finally toleration for these qualities or attributes when exemplified in his contemporaries.'

But to me this most true and excellent summary is spoilt by the fact that all these qualities are (typically) enumerated under the heading of The qualities which Mr. Alfred Noyes has not got. Now I hold no brief for Mr. Alfred Noyes, and I am not sure that I do not from time to time agree with Mr. Monro's opening paragraph about him:

'Of Alfred Noyes nothing can be written in extenuation.'

but Mr. Monro's bitterness defeats its own object and the reader, of course, begins to sympathise with Mr. Noyes.

A very different critic is Mrs. Marguerite Wilkinson, an American. She, like Mr. Sturge Moore, never mixes up criticism and controversy. Her book 'New Voices' is intended as a more or less elementary introduction to modern poetry. It is all suavity and good sense. Mrs. Wilkinson can blame without being severe, can see faults and virtues in the same set of verses, and is an admirable analyst. The reader will find an extract from her book in the chapter on Metre. The passage consists of some observations on Miss Amy Lowell's 'Patterns,' and will, I think, display Mrs. Wilkinson's virtues as well as her one vice. This vice is that she is so interested in technique, she understands the poets she is criticising so well, that she is apt to be a little too charitable, and in the case of a good many American writers she is apt to take the will for the deed, and to treat mediocrity with a respect only due to first-rate powers. This, of course, weakens her book. But, as I have said, she possesses in a high degree the power of analysis; she really knows how to concentrate on a poem and to consider it under several headings, which is, as anyone who has tried it knows, as difficult as trout-tickling. She also possesses the faculty for putting a book together and knows when to give the reader ample quotations and to allow him to judge for himself.

Mr. Hueffer's 'Thus to Revisit,' though it is not solely concerned with poetry, will in many passages give the reader a very good idea of one tendency of modern criticism. Mr. Hueffer has, of course, a considerable acquaintance with French and German literature, and therefore brings back to the study of his countrymen very useful detached judgment. I think that the main lesson he has to teach English writers is the central notion of the classical writer—I mean consideration for the reader.

Mr. Robert Graves represents perhaps the newest type of critic of all. He analyses, but he is also a mystic, and to my mind his book 'On English Poetry' is one of the most valuable and suggestive critical essays that has ever appeared. Unlike many poets, he writes prose delightfully, and his all too short book is extraordinarily readable.

It suffers perhaps from one fault: it is too much a series of hints, and too little a sustained statement, but Mr. Graves himself disarms this criticism by saying that his book is material for critics to work upon, not a ready-made criticism. It is an effort to display the workings of a poet's mind, rather than the exposition of a critical theory. Really, of course, the whole standpoint of the book, the mating of criticism to psychology, is in itself a contribution to aesthetic theory.

No one interested either in psychology or poetry ought to miss Mr. Graves' book. His readers will see that it has a good many points in common with the present work. This, is in most cases the result of coincidence, but in the case of certain notions in the chapter on Symbolism and in the general conception of Metre and Rhythm as intellectual anodynes, I gratefully own myself Mr. Graves' debtor.

CHAPTER XX

PARODIES, SATIRES AND EPIGRAMS

I WISH that a course of good parody were compulsory for aspirant poets. Parody has the advantage over criticism that all art has over didactics. By reading parodies or witnessing Macbeth a dissatisfaction either with murders or *clichés*, as the case may be, is made to spring within the breast of the would-be poet or murderer. The preacher and the reviewer only apply pressure from without and are generally met by an exactly equivalent internal resistance. Luckily we have a very flourishing modern tradition in this kind. Not all the vituperation in the world could deal with what we might call the 'Classical Inadequate School' as finally as did 'J.B.M.,' author of 'Georgeous Poetry,' in half-a-dozen lines :

'The blackbird's gay November song
And the primroses scattered far
Fill all the sky with lutes and bells
From star to frosty star.
Beside the pond the pipit cries,
The heather's all abloom,
The winter sun among the sedge
Weaves and unweaves its loom.'

Or consider Mr. Squire and the 'exquisite' sonnet. There is Time's acolyte palely frustrating the sunset.

'No purple mars the chalice; not a bird
Shrills o'er the solemn silence of thy fame.'

But, of course, the robuster the poet the more exhilarating the parody. There is 'J.B.M.'s' notion of—I suppose—Mr. Chesterton. It begins like this:

'Babies have such little toes,
So soft and pink and small:
"Four by six," said the master-plumber,
And I worked at my wall.
Babies have such innocent ways,
So quiet and nice and sweet;
"Get that pipe laid down there, 'Arry,"
I work that they may eat.
Babies and I will be dust one day,
What's the good of it all?
"One yard out," said the master-plumber,
Leaning against the wall.'

Then there are Mr. Vachel Lindsay and Mr. Masefield. Mr. E. V. Knox conceived the pleasant notion of writing about Lord Northcliffe first in the style of one and then of the other.

'Old Man Alf was an ink proprietor;
His voice was loud and never grew quieter;
He kept rude scribes in a monstrous den
To hammer on a gong at Cabinet men.
Hark to Mail-horn, rail-horn, sale-horn,
Boomlay, boomlay, boomlay, boomlay, boom!
Listen to the Times-horn, chimes-horn, crimes-horn,
Boomlay, boomlay, boomlay, boomlay, boom!
Pom, bing, pom!
(With a touch of "Alexander's Ragtime Band").'

Upon which the parodist turns to Mr. Lloyd George as 'Daniel' in the same vein.

The huntsman, Alfred, rode The Mail,
A bright bay mount, his best of prancers,
Out of Forget-me-not by Answers,

A thick-set man was Alf, and hard,
He chewed a straw from the stable-yard:
He owned a chestnut, The Dispatch,
With one white sock, and one white patch;
He bred the mare called Comic Cuts;
He was a man with fearful guts.

So, too, was Rother, the first whip,
Nothing could give this man the pip;
He rode The Mirror, a raking horse,
A piebald full of points and force.
All that was best in English life,
All that appealed to man or wife,
Sweet peas or standard bread or sales
These two men loved. They hated Wales - - -

The Lloyd George motive is again heard, this time he is, of course, under the fox's mask. I have quoted this Masefieldian essay because it provides an instance of a thing which not uncommonly happens in this sort of writing. Can the reader see what is wrong with this parody? If not, here is another example of the trouble, also by Mr. E. V. Knox. This time Mr. de la Mare is to be parodied:

' " Won't you look out for your Fleet, Mr. Bull? '
Quoth the Navy, nigging, nagging in the papers:
" Can't you look out for your Fleet, Mr. Bull?"
Quoth the Navy, shouting madly in the papers.'

The fact is that in neither of these two cases has Mr. Knox written a parody at all. The poems are really both of them direct satires about English public events, and not indirect comments on the style of two poets. The poems have transmuted themselves. The centre of interest has shifted from manner to matter. Not but what Direct Satire can be a very good thing:

> 'Yet let me flap this bug with gilded wings,
> This painted child of dirt, that stinks and stings;
> Whose buzz the witty and the fair annoys,
> Yet wit ne'er tastes, and beauty ne'er enjoys:
> So well-bred spaniels civilly delight
> In mumbling of the game they dare not bite.
> Eternal smiles his emptiness betray,
> As shallow streams run dimpling all the way.
>
> . . . . . .
>
> His wit all see-saw, between that and this,
> Now high, now low, now master up, now miss,
> And he himself one vile antithesis.
> Amphibious thing! that acting either part,
> The trifling head or the corrupted heart,
> Fop at the toilet, flatterer at the board,
> Now trips a lady, and now struts a lord.
>
> . . . . . .
>
> Beauty that shocks you, parts that none will trust;
> Wit that can creep, and pride that licks the dust.'

It is rather odd, I think, that the present age does not produce more and better verse in this manner. Mr. Kipling's very striking 'Gahaizi' and Mr. Squire's 'Survival of the Fittest' seem almost the only successful modern poems in this tradition. War satires, of course, we have had in plenty, but these I count as too impersonal to come into this category. On the whole, however, perhaps Indirect Ironical Satire is a better weapon. Consider, for instance, the last lines of the 'Dunciad,' when, her speech at an end at last, the Goddess nods:

> 'The all-composing hour
> Resistless falls: the Muse obeys the pow'r.

She comes! she comes! the sable throne behold
Of Night primeval and of Chaos old!
Before her, Fancy's gilded clouds decay,
And all its varying rainbows die away.
Wit shoots in vain its momentary fires,
The meteor drops, and in a flash expires.
As one by one, at dread Medea's strain,
The sick'ning stars fade off th' ethereal plain;

. . . . . .

See skulking Truth to her old cavern fled,
Mountains of casuistry heaped o'er her head!
Philosophy, that leaned on Heaven before,
Shrinks to her second cause, and is no more.
Physic of Metaphysic begs defence,
And Metaphysic calls for aid on sense!
See Mystery to Mathematics fly!
In vain! they gaze, turn giddy, rave and die.
Religion, blushing veils her sacred fires,
And unawares Morality expires.
For public flame, nor private, dare to shine;
Nor human spark is left, nor glimpse divine!
Lo: thy dread empire, Chaos! is restored;
Light dies before thy uncreating word;
Thy hand, great Anarch! lets the curtain fall;
And universal darkness buries all.'

Again here the present age has not so far done much. Mr. Augustine Rivers essayed a little in the Dunciad vein in the Sixth Cycle of Wheels, calling his poem, 'The Death of Mercury.' The goddesses Dullness and Mediocrity are progressing slow and magnificent to their thrones:

'And as, in state, they to their temple go,
They hymn "Praise Squire from whom all blessings flow,
Oh, may he prosper! May his brood increase,
And death to all who are not Dull as he is!"
Up from glad Earth the chorus swells again,
"Praise Squire, Praise Squire," we hear the swift refrain

That leaps like fire from every school and college,
From stately London home or Cotswold Cottage
Wherever poet meets a poet brother
(Or makes an income by reviewing each other.)
The echo alters to "We never tire
Of hearing Squire on Shanks and Shanks on Squire."'

The goddesses (pursues the satirist) are indeed merely showing a proper sense of gratitude. For it was for them that he cast aside, 'The gift of parody his only art,' for them that in secret lair he fashioned 'the gummy, muddy "Lily of Malud."' He and his 'foursquare' henchmen, Freeman, Turner, Graves, Shanks and 'reckless' Rickword, are eternally vowed to her service—and so on. None of it is quite as well polished, either in point of satire or of versification, as it ought to be. For Messrs. Turner and Graves may have faults, they might be accused of being unduly obscure, mystic and rhapsodical, but to lump them all together as dull reminds us of the angry aimlessness of the banderlogue.

The fact is, that when we turn from Parody to Satire we are too often obliged to turn away from humour. I am not going here to attempt to define humour, but I believe with Mr. Robert Graves, that it is somehow pretty closely allied to the subconscious, mystical element in aesthetics. I should fancy that humour was, in fact, like the arts, a channel by which two subconsciousnesses were able to communicate. In nonsense and in jokes we are often aware of the same sort of sense of liberation and pleasure as in reading good poetry. And that is why I think that the more amusing and the less severe Parody, Satire and Epigram can remain, the nearer they are to poetry. Savage, denunciatory satire should stick to prose forms. 'Gulliver's Travels' would have lost a great deal by being written in verse. But, of course, neither Parody nor Epigram need altogether divorce themselves from malice. Only the *jeu d'esprit* should on the whole leave a pleasant flavour, and there should remain to the reader a slight sense of adventure.

> 'Bees and epigrams should
> If they are not to fail
> Have honey, small frames,
> And a sting in the tail.'

Quite pleasant examples of this classical type of epigram are to be found among the works of Mr. C. L. Graves. For instance, here is one which depends on verbal felicity:

> 'The grocer who has made his pile
> Does he grow nicer? No, sir.
> He does not change his heart or style,
> And grows a grosser grocer.'

Mr. Graves' work is, of course, in direct descent from the excellent school of epigram that flourished in Oxford about forty years ago and included so vast a literature on Mr. Jowett. I have always liked the verse about the pathetic Don who—unwillingly—helped Jowett with an immense translation:

> 'Oh, I say! I once was Forbes,
> Now the Master me absorbs
> Me and many other me's
> In his vast Thucydides.'

But there are Gothic as well as Classic epigrams. And in their wild fashion they are quite as difficult to write :

> ' Edward the Confessor
> Slept under the dresser,
> When that began to pall
> He slept in the hall.'

That is perhaps the archetypal Gothic epigram. Now observe a classic mind struggling to use the form :

> ' The Emperor Nero
> Was not a Christian Hero
> He used Communicants
> As illuminants.'

Brilliant, but too intellectual ! It lacks abandon and reminds the reader of the river front of the Houses of Parliament.

But with the Gothic epigram the reader will perceive that we have almost got round to poetry again. Our actual way of return would, of course, be *via* Nursery Rhymes, Edward Lear and Messrs. Robert Graves and Walter de la Mare.

Will the reader allow me two more modern instances of the art of Parody; the first is by Ezra Pound and mocks generally at the grandiloquents :

> ' When I behold how black, immortal ink
> Drips from my deathless pen—ah, well-away !
> Why should we stop at all for what I think?
> There is enough in what I chance to say.'

The second is another of Mr. Knox's efforts. It is from a poem called ' Glamour.' I beg the reader to turn to the end of the book where, under Mr.

W. J. Turner's name, he will find quotations from the original, 'Paris and Helen.'

'Huge was the hall, and principally made
Of porphyry, alabaster, bronze and jade,
And noteworthy for its large dining-room.
Paris, a guest within the oblonged gloom,
Where all the cups were carved with col'd pure shapes
Of boys and maidens eating unripe grapes,
Gazed upon Helen. All Troy's hope was pawned
In that one love-look. Menelaus yawned.'

And those who are familiar with Mr. Turner's poem will enjoy another couplet:

'Hoary with age and antique with old Time
The walls of Troy stood difficult to climb.'

Nor shall we like it the less because by it we are reminded of a really admirable passage in the original. Did anyone ever enjoy his Wordsworth or a ballad the less because of Canning or Calverley? It is a great thing that the new school of poetry should have bred so likely a school of parody. No Government can exist without an Opposition. Poets fall into absurdities unless they are criticised, and of all criticism parody is probably the most effective and the least offensive. It is like the parable in the world of ethics—it does not rouse a spirit of opposition in the individual criticised. The study it shows of the poet's work even turns it into a kind of wry compliment. A poet can accept its hints without loss of *amour-propre*. Many of us dislike being told that we are getting fat, but few of us are so ill-tempered that we should frown at the distorting glass that tells us so with disarming exaggeration.

PART V
(FOR READERS)

SHORT STUDIES OF SOME MODERN POETS

D. H. LAWRENCE

In Mr. Lawrence the novelist, and still more the philosopher, was always inclined to shoulder out the poet. Of late the poet had seemed entirely ousted, but in a poem which appeared in *The Mercury* in the Autumn of 1921, called 'The Snake,' he re-asserted himself. Mr. Lawrence has had considerable influence upon other modern writers, and it is therefore not uninteresting to try and estimate his contribution to modern lyrical poetry.

In reading Mr. Lawrence's poems we shall probably in the first place be struck by their vigour. The emotional stress is often tremendous. We feel that the content is always bursting out of the skin of the poem. The inspiration was apparently, as a rule, too white-hot to submit to the bonds of a regular metre. Often there was not even time for any symbolism. The poem is a naked, direct statement. Take the following, 'Lot's Wife.' It seems devoid of every quality that we expect in verse, except emotion, and yet who can deny it the title of poetry?

I have seen it, felt it in my mouth, my throat, my chest,
my belly,

Burning of powerful salt, burning, eating through my defenceless nakedness,
I have been thrust into white sharp crystals,
Writhing, twisting, superpenetrated,
Ah, Lot's wife, Lot's wife!
The pillar of salt, the whirling, horrible column of salt, like a waterspout
That has enveloped me!

This directness often gives to the poems a curious flavour that we associate with very different productions—Mr. Waley's exquisite translations from the Chinese. They have the same naked simplicity, but the Chinese poets have come to it not from stress and agony of emotion, but from niceness and satiety, and a taste purged and refined through the centuries.

What do we have to pay for this tensity, this veritable vibration, in Mr. Lawrence? As we should expect, his poems, or rather his mental attitude, seem to be without sense of proportion.

He is, of course, a psychologist of great merit, but when we find him in the sickroom of suffering humanity, his rôle seems to be that of the patient rather than that of the physician or the enquiring scientist. But before we condemn his methods of expression, we must remember how difficult are the things which he is trying to express and how tremendous to him is their emotional stress. Sex is a subject upon which few of us—Councillor Clark or Mr. Lawrence—can write calmly. Mr. Lawrence is struggling so hard to give utterance to some burning emotion that his verse often becomes tortured and harsh—a contortion rather than a poem. The more violent the emotion of which he writes, the more we are conscious of a febrile quality in the verse. He can never stand back from his passion. Therefore we often find that his most passionate love poetry, remarkable as it is, is so feverish as to be pathology, not literature. We have perhaps been moved and duly caught into the swing of the poet's mood, and then Mr. Lawrence allows his high temperature to get the better of him, and lets himself slip into what is something very near to delirium—too near, at any rate, to be expressed in half a dozen lines. I wonder if he would be able to say what he wanted in an epic or a poetic drama? It is not impossible. As it is we find the paradox that Mr. Lawrence often writes best upon what are to him emphatically secondary subjects. Two poems about children in *Amores*, for instance, are extraordinarily beautiful and well observed, especially perhaps the one which begins.—

> 'When the bare feet of the baby beat across the grass
> The little white feet nod like white flowers in the wind,'

and which ends.—

> 'I long for the baby to wander hither to me
> Like a wind-shadow wandering over the water,
> So that she can stand on my knee
> With her little bare feet in my hands,
> Cool like syringa buds,
> Firm and silken like pink young peony flowers.'

'The Snake' not only contains fine lines but is most effective as a whole.

But whatever may be Mr. Lawrence's faults, this poem of the baby illustrates his chief virtue. He is rarely negligible. His poems have an intense objective existence. To borrow a most repulsive expression from the jargon of the stage, they are always 'strong.' There appears to be no civilised expression which gives the notion conveyed by the phrase, 'Punch back of it.' And yet this is a quality of which we are particularly conscious in poetry. There are delightful poets whose works are singularly wraith-like. Their poems may be admirable and charming, but we feel that they are akin to Herrick's daffodils and fade away so fast that we must use a sort of cunning in relation to them—must stalk them. *Per contra*, there are poems which we may like much less; they are often dull or unsubtle, for instance, but which are irrevocable. This vigorous life belongs, in a high degree, to Mr. Lawrences poetry. It is this lesson of strength that he has to impart to younger writers.

ROBERT GRAVES

I AM not going to say very much in this book about Mr. Robert Graves as a poet. There are two Mr. Robert Graves', and they now both stand revealed in his books. When I say that there are two, I merely mean that you can like his poetry for its under or its upper meaning. You can like the work of the writer of nursery rhymes with a sneaking or a patronising affection, as you prefer; or you can be repelled or attracted by the mystic and the prophet and the impish, fantastic humourist. For Mr. Graves' real character I must refer the reader to 'The Pier Glass,' 'Country Sentiment,' and the book to which the present volume owes so much, 'On English Poetry.'

I propose to say nothing of his real attitude towards poetry, an attitude with which I am in fundamental, indeed almost in detailed agreement. This attitude is more accurately shown in the texture of this book where it is displayed in many of its applications, than it would be possible to express it in a sentence or two. There is only one piece of advice that I should give to the reader, and that is (contrary to the wise procedure with most poets), to read Mr. Graves' theory before his practice. This because, like other writers, he has published a good many bad poems. He has not always realised in writing and publishing his verse the cases in which an individual poem proved to have a leak, where the mystical contents which he put into it has run away, and only appears to him to be still there because he knows he put it there. Now a reader looking for beauty easily 'spots' an ugly poem—a failure—but to look in a perfectly dark room for a symbolical black cat which isn't there is proverbially disillusioning. Then he is occasionally obscure, giving us enough plot to distract us from the writing, but making that plot indecipherably involved and fantastic. An example to my mind of this sort of failure is 'The Gnat.' I got that poem expounded to me by Mr. Graves, and when you are given a clue, you find it is far from being the unsatisfactory affair that the unaided reader is likely to find it. But there it stands in 'The Pier Glass' unexplained, and, I honestly believe to most people, incomprehensible.

But Mr. Graves does not often fail, for he is a very good poet indeed. I should like to quote to the reader 'Black Horse Lane' as an excellent and typical example of Mr. Graves' genius. Here we have the top meaning of nursery rhyme, and the fantastic under-meaning bringing with it wide implications,—generalising the message of the poet as only works of art which employ the symbolic method can. Dame Jane is a music mistress and Sharkie is the baker. One day a fiddle tunes up, Starkie catches up Jane and they fly out of the lane 'like swallows.' But nobody knew what he said to her, nobody saw how she looked.

'. . . . .

No neighbour heard
One sigh or one word,
Not a sound but the fiddling in Black Horse Lane,
The happy noise of music—
Again and again.

Where now be those two old 'uns,
be those two old 'uns,
Sharkie the baker run off with Jane?
Hark ye up to Flint Street,
Halloo to Pepper-Mint Street,
Follow by the fells to the great North Plain,
By the fells and the river—
To the cold North Plain.

How came this passion to them,
this passion to them,
Love in a freshet on Black Horse Lane?
It came without warning
One blue windy morning

So they scarcely might know was it joy or pain,
With scarce breath to wonder—
Was it joy or pain.

Took they no fardels with them,
no fardels with them.
Out and alone on the ice-bound plain?
Sharkie he had rockets
And crackers in his pockets,
Ay, and she had a plaid shawl to keep off the rain,
An old Highland plaid shawl—
To keep off the rain.'

When you have read Mr. Graves' critical book, then patronise that poem if you still dare. But indeed only the pedant would desire to do that. There is something as fresh and disarming in Mr. Graves' fantasy as there is profound in his psychology.

STURGE MOORE.

To me Mr. Sturge Moore is a source of perennial interest as being an endless experimentor in form. His resource in this one respect seems infinite.

The amphibious form, the book, which is written half in verse, half in prose, is one with which he is always toying. It is always an attractive form to the writer, though most poets are, not unwisely, afraid of its too great freedom. By employing this style the poet can suit his form to the several parts of his theme. He has a sense of the elasticity of a mixed medium. But I am not quite sure if such a mixture is often a success from the reader's point of view. *The Pilgrim's Progress* gains immensely by the careful skipping of its fortunately infrequent verse. Alfred's *Boethius* is little adorned by its metrical portions. Sir James Barrie's *The Truth about the Russian Dancers*—half play, half ballet—proved dramatic cross-breds to be not less difficult creatures to manage than literary amphibians. There are conventions in our enjoyment of every art. Convention prevents our even desiring to encircle with a finger the pillars in a Claude. We feel no disappointment because we cannot satisfy touch. But let parts of a landscape be modelled in high relief and the flat portions which are left will annoy us.

We do not resent, we scarcely apprehend, as unnatural, the metric speech of the characters in a narrative poem. But let some of the persons speak in prose and we are critical where we should have acquiesced. So perhaps it comes about that the reader has a feeling that he is not being quite fair to the scholarly spirit and many beauties of Mr. Sturge Moore's *The Powers of the Air*. For not only is *The Powers of the Air* half in verse and half in prose, but it is half image and half argument. It is a Socratic dialogue in which the scene—light, shade, colour, gesture, sound and scent— is as prominent as the exposition of general principles. The visualization is excellent, the dialogue well knit, even if the argument is not very masculine; the characterization is clear, the verse generally melodious, the prose often beautiful. The *ensemble* is interesting without for a moment touching the heart or the imagination. The effects are somehow dissipated. We trip over the several conventions. In another volume, 'Danae and Blind Thamyris,' he tells the story of Charon's 'select academy for the sons of heroes.' It is pleasing, but I for one do not feel that Mr. Moore has even here proved that verse and decorative prose can make up a whole. But this is only one of Mr. Moore's formal experiments. In another volume, 'Tragic Mothers,' 'Three short plays for chamber presentation,' he makes a gallant effort to write a drama for 'three voices heard behind a screen.' It begins well, but Niobi's long soliloquy would probably be intensely dull from an invisible speaker with no help of gesture.

But Mr. Sturge Moore has the merits of his defects. If his work occasionally drops into listlessness, it does not descend further into inadequacy. It is mellow and reflective, and is always easy, agreeable reading. He has a pretty eye for colour, for landscape, and an understanding of one aspect of the female mind. With his mildness he always retains a certain scholarly distinction—he does not, in Jenny Pearl's phrase, become 'soppy.' He has a mind which in many ways resembles that of Matthew Arnold, only he is without much of the Victorian's irritation at a world full of vulgar numskulls.

The dedication of a narrative poem, 'Aforetime,' to Mr. Gordon Bottomley gives a capital picture of a mellow and reflective mind at work fashioning verses with a sort of cool affection :

> 'Dear exile from the hurrying crowd,
> At work I muse to you aloud ;

Thought on my anvil softens, glows,
And I forget our art has foes;
For life, the mother of beauty, seems
A joyous sleep with waking dreams.
Then the toy armoury of the brain
Opining, judging, looks as vain
As trowels silver gilt for use
Of mayors and kings, who have to lay
Foundation stones in hope they may
Be honoured for walls others build.
I, in amicable muse,
With fathomless wonder only filled,
Whisper over to your ear
Listening two hundred odd miles north,
And give thought chase that, were you here,
Our talk would never run to earth.'

Perhaps he is at his best when, as in Danae, he is turning a sometimes lewd old story to 'favour and to prettiness.' To borrow his own words,

'Leaves wet with dew in lettuce-hearts confined,
Are not more dainty or more clear of hue.'

Such is this tale. Perhaps the best thing he ever wrote is another play from 'Tragic Mothers,' called 'Medea.' I am not quite sure of its absolute merit, part of its attraction to me being its ingenuity.

'A curtain bearer and two curtain folders' play the ingeniously conceived parts of mediums at a *séance* and Chorus. Medea has sacrificed her two sons to appease Artemis, who was wroth at her broken vow of chastity. She hunts once more in the train of the goddess, but is haunted by the thought of the two boys for whose forgiveness she longs. She invokes them, and they speak to her through the lips of the entranced chorus. She begs them to understand her deed. She killed them that they might escape bondage, but her heart is torn at the thought of her cruelty. The voices are silent, and she fears that grief or anger keeps them so. But she has forgotten that they are children. They are playing hide-and-seek:

'MERMEROS:
I said: "Now we must hide," but Pheres said:
"She cannot see us, there's no need to hide."
Then I said: "Hide from hearing, hide in silence,
We'll not be found there till she makes us laugh."

PHERES:
That's the new hide-and-seek we play at now.

MEDEA (incredulously):
But are you really there? You move about?

BOTH BOYS:
Yes, we are here, and run and leap and laugh.

MEDEA (kneeling on one knee and holding out her arms):
Come, I have much to whisper, heart to heart.

MERMEROS:
What a beautiful bow you've got.

PHERES: Bend it, mother.

MEDEA:
I want your pardon, you can only give it
When you shall know how cruel were the wrongs . . . .

BOTH BOYS (interrupting):
Shoot, mother, shoot.'

Again she tries to ease her heavy conscience, but only succeeds in making the children cry, and when she desists, hopeless, they tell her how the rabbits do not fear them now. They talk of childish things and break her heart afresh. Well played, the little scene might be extremely poignant.

GORDON BOTTOMLEY.

Mr. Gordon Bottomley is the only serious English exponent of the verse drama, and in his best productions he follows the lead neither of Maeterlinck, nor of the Irish school. There is always a danger in the Maeterlincken drama of the sort of thing that Mr. Squire parodies so attractively (in 'Collected Parodies').

> 'From the forest on the left SIX OLD MEN enter. The five of them are blind and deaf and dumb, but the sixth is not dumb. He is only blind and deaf. They walk very slowly and stumblingly. The first feels his way with his staff. The others also feel their ways with their staffs, tripping over sticks and dead leaves as they go.'

The 'Belgian Shakespeare' has much to answer for.

In bad examples of the Celtic school we get another sort of absurdity, a kind of stark, tremendous heroism all about nothing, and both schools are apt to suffer from that besetting trouble of the poetic drama—a lack of vigour. Mr. Gordon Bottomley has his faults, but in two or three plays he has avoided these pitfalls. The best of his dramas have a strength and a vigour which is immediately striking to the reader, and—in the only one that I have had the pleasure of seeing acted, 'King Lear's Wife'—these qualities were equally apparent to a theatre audience.

Two of Mr. Bottomley's plays are concerned with the past of Shakespearian characters—'King

Lear's Wife' and 'Grauch.' King Lear is shown us as a still vigorous, middle-aged man; his wife is dying.

In M. Komisarjevsky's production of the play a great bed was mounted on a platform, its head against the back of the stage, and six or eight steps on the three sides led up to this couch. It was an admirable symbolic device. The queen, isolated and alone, yet dominates the situation. The King has fallen in love with one of her young waiting women who should be nursing her. But Lear is always luring the willing Gormflaith from her sleeping mistress. The Queen does not quite know what is going on, but she suspects, and we are given a wonderful picture of her despair largely through the mouth of the doctor who attends her.

'PHYSICIAN: We cannot die wholly against our wills;
And in the texture of women I have found
Harder determination than in men:
The body grows impatient of enduring,
The harried mind is from the body estranged,
And we consent to go: by the Queen's touch,
The way she moves—or does not move—in bed,
The eyes so cold and keen in her white mask,
I know she has consented.'

The characters of the two elder daughters, Goneril and Regan, are also admirably portrayed.

Goneril draws her own portrait at length for us—cold, pure, ruthless—and then shows us the sordid Regan:

'I dreamt that I was swimming, shoulder up,
And drave the bedclothes spreading to the floor:
Coldness awoke me; through the waning darkness
I heard far hounds give shivering aëry tongue,

Remote, withdrawing, suddenly faint and near,
I leapt and saw a pack of stretching weasels
Hunt a pale coney in a soundless rush.
Their elfin and thin yelping pierced my heart
As with an unseen beauty long awaited;
Wolf-skin and cloak I buckled over this night-gear,
And took my honoured spear from my bed-side
Where none but I may touch its purity,
And sped as lightly down the dewy bank
As any mothy owl that hunts quick mice.
They went crying, crying, but I lost them
Before I stept, with the first tips of light,
On Raven Crag near by the Druid Stones . . .'

. . . .

'Does Regan worship anywhere at dawn?'
The sweaty half-clad cook-maids render lard
Out in the scullery, after pig-killing,
And Regan sidles among their greasy skirts,
Smeary and hot as they, for craps to suck.
I lost my thoughts before the giant Stones . . .
And when anew the earth assembled round me
I swung out on the heath and woke a hare
And speared it at a cast and shouldered it.'

But Mr. Bottomley has his faults. We can see them large in 'Midsummer Eve.' Stage directions matter very much in a poetic drama. It is difficult to lay down rules for their proper conceiving. Such plays, it must be remembered, are intended both to be read and acted. But has the poet clearly envisaged either group of his disciples in the following?

'All is soundless again save for the cow's moaning. The twilight deepens no farther, and presently its dead gold brownness becomes cooler in tone; the mist which had been merged in the nightfall's dimness, imperceptibly becomes apparent again, being suffused by an oozing of silveriness through the pervading brownness; moon-rise is evident, although the moon is hidden by the permeating mist which it fills. Perhaps a crying of bats is heard, but this is not certain. An owl cries somewhere—probably from one of the gable-holes, for it sounds both inside and outside at once; after many tentative Tu-whits it launches a full Tu-whoo and swings out far and low across the valley: a chirping of frogs begins in the nearest ditches. . . .'

The rest is obviously legitimate, for it consists of directions as to the position of the characters. But in the above passage, what purpose is achieved or intended? It is surely neither a hint on interpretation to the actors, a guide to the proper management of the limes and the conduct of the 'property' bats, nor is it a piece of prose whose cadence is to vary the blank verse for the reader.

However, we very rarely find Mr. Gordon Bottomley 'talking through his hat' like this; his plays are usually models of economy and restraint.

'Grauch,' like 'King Lear's Wife,' is an attempt to reconstruct the past of one of Shakespeare's characters.

This time he has chosen Lady Macbeth. She is a girl and is to be married (because her lands march with his) to the oafish but good-natured Thane of Fortingall, the owner of 'a small, black stone castle in the north of Scotland.' It is the eve of her wedding to this bridegroom, whose state and character she views with equal contempt. The scene opens with the wedding preparations, a device which automatically answers the reader's question, 'Why should she marry him unless she chose?'

by showing the reiterated pressure of minor commonplace events on the strongest character.

The question of whether Grauch shall marry the Thane of Fortingall is completely buried under the question of how many guests are to be expected, who is to skin the rabbits and pluck the game for the wedding feast, and how the embroidery of Grauch's wedding-dress is to be finished in time. All this is true. Who does not know in everyday life the extraordinary power of the lesser to contain the greater?

Exhausted by these small cares, the family are just going to bed when the King's envoy, on his way to Inverness, knocks and demands stable and lodging. It is the young Macbeth. The envoy and to-morrow's bride fall immediately in love with one another, and in another sleep-walking scene this love is declared. Almost at once the girl, though she is never the mature, assured woman that Shakespeare drew, begins to dominate the fiery but impressionable Macbeth. He carries her off with him, and her last act is to make him swear that one day he will come back and burn the home that has sheltered her in revenge for the fact that here her will was nearly bent to that of others.

In 'Britain's Daughter' Mr. Bottomley partly re-tells the story of Trojan Women, except that here the moral is not quite so plain as is Euripides'. The Britons under their Queen, the mother of the heroine, 'Nest,' have risen against the Roman rule. Nest is an eaglet, a true primitive fighter with the clear code of the warrior and the fierce virginal character of Mr. Bottomley's Goneril, but she is ennobled by a real patriotic flame. Of the miseries which this patriotism has brought about, the 'common people' in the play complain. There are the childless old women, the girls driven off as a prey to the soldiers, the starving children, the spitted babies of Troy and of Belgium and of Russia. As in 'Trojan Women,' the stage is during a great part of the action illuminated by the light of burning dwellings.

Psychologically the merit of the play is that it shows us how the primitive virtues almost inevitably bring this sort of thing about.

The play is full of life and interest. Mr. Bottomley cares both for subtle psychological states and the most primitive sensations of bodily wants. Compare these two passages, which in the play follow almost immediately upon one another:

'THE SECOND WOMAN:
The cold strikes through my shoes; even on the sands
The rime is thick. The rime will settle on us,
The frost will reach our bone-pith before dawn comes.
I shall have a stiff stomach for a week.

'THE THIRD WOMAN:
You should have brought two cloaks.

'THE SECOND WOMAN:
My house is full of drunken Roman men
Who throw their arms around my empty mead-vat.

'THE FIRST WOMAN:
At the top of the street I passed a dead woman
Wearing good clothes. I pared off her skirt and leg-cloths,
And donned them over my own. . . .'

Madron is one of Nest's subjects, goaded by his miseries into abuse of the young captive Queen and an attack upon her as she stands bound to a post by the quayside. She has defied him:

'MADRON:
I have not seen such mettle in a girl,
My lasses are flinchers and wheedlers and all for themselves.
Delicate meats, soft clothing and warm fur,
The eagerness of hunting, and gold that frees
From long toil and subservience, seem to breed
A generous and daring of spirit
That more might share if more were favoured so.
Maiden, the keenness of your soul can hurt,
Though not your pride of state, not your steeled mind:
Life is fair and an opening wonder in you:
I will not touch you; I will serve life in you,
Though not your state, if you will tell your need. . . .'

I think that we should place the two dramas in 'Grauch' and 'Britain's Daughter' after 'King Lear's Wife,' but before 'The Riding to Lithend' and 'Midsummer Eve.'

Has the reader observed from the extracts I have given how carefully he has been spared any monotony in the run of the metre. How well Mr. Bottomley has diversified his blank verse. His metrical devices are never obtrusive, but almost invariably effective. I am not sure if Mr. Bottomley's work (excepting 'King Lear's Wife') has great monumental value in itself. (Whether it will be read in twenty years' time, for example.) I do, however, think that it has great interest for his contemporaries as marking a definite stage in the elucidation of the problems presented by the poetic drama. His work is valuable not only for its positive merits, but as a standing proof that it is possible in poetic drama to avoid the chief faults of the Irish and Maeterlinckian schools. Mr. Squire has pointed out that essentially what Maeterlinck did was to invent a dramatic version of the '*Fin de siècle*' lyric. The Irish school have something of the same taking tricks of method, the same triviality of matter. Both are rather oppressed by the solution of problems of technique and grow self-conscious in the performance of what they feel to be acrobatic feats. Mr. Bottomley seems to take the writing of poetic drama quite naturally as a perfectly obvious form of human activity.

A careful study of his work will save the young dramatist from a great many errors and absurdities.

W. J. TURNER.

MOST of Mr. Turner's shorter pieces have a certain quality which it is difficult to name. To me they recall the image of a black opal. This simile suggests itself partly, because he does actually often describe dark, sombre colours and burning glowing lights, and partly because there is often the same quality of fire in the poems themselves, a quality at once elusive and a little menacing. All the clear, everyday gaiety and charm of which Mr. Turner is capable, he seems to have put entirely on one side, and when he chooses to give it to the public, he gives it unadulterated by 'The Dark Fire' of his shorter pieces.

I am not quite sure that the definite separation between his two styles is a good thing. 'Paris and Helen' is sometimes so clear as to produce an effect of shallowness while the less successful of the short pieces are occasionally tortured and incomprehensible. At his best, however, Mr. Turner can make a success of both methods.

'Paris and Helen' has one quality which I for one esteem highly in a narrative poem. It is agreeable and easy to read. The versification carries you along like the easy current of a stream. I have one grievance in the earlier part of the poem. The reader is scarcely allowed a glimpse of the affair of the apple. It is very disappointing, as we had hoped for a fine set piece from Mr. Turner. However, we are partly consoled by a capital thunderstorm, during which two messengers come up from Troy to tell Paris that he is wanted. Their dark cloaks flap in the yellow light of the great storm clouds. The ship and the fatal voyage which take Paris to Greece are shown with an admirably contrived sense of enchantment and mystery about them. The ship has 'a painted Amor' carved on her prow which is caressed by the 'sea-wandering airs'—a truly Homeric epithet.

When it comes to Helen herself, we are again treated shabbily as in the matter of the Judgment. 'The face that launched a thousand ships' is scarcely described: we see only her 'wild, calm beauty' as it is mirrored in the eyes of the men who gaze at her. But perhaps the best thing in the book is the description of Troy set in its ramparts, when Paris brings back his paramour. There stand the huge outer walls of Troy, 'like some sublime sea-wrack':—

> 'Enormous age has smoothed her stones away,
> And the soft, giant hands of Night and Day
> Have crumbled mountain dust upon her walls.'

Then Priam and his lords sitting in council are described:—

> 'Not a sound
> Disturbed the solemn, century-laden air.'

The Council Hall is magnificent and barbaric with 'the spoils of ancient wars,' and the old lords are on their seats of gold:—

> 'Who sat bejewelled grasping their jewelled swords.'

At last the doors are flung open:—

> 'There stood Prince Paris with his heavenly bride.
> Upon King Priam and those silent lords
> Then fell the glance that drew ten thousand swords
> To flash on Ilion. Slowly in that blaze
> The Phrygian Princes rose.'

The end of the story is told in the same sort of way; all is made fair and mystical, a scene out of a huge languid drama.

What could be in greater contrast to these large clear prospects than a poem like 'The Caves of Auvergne.' Primitive man back from the wars carves with a sort of sombre exultation images of deer and bull on the smooth walls of the cave.

> 'The stars flew by the cave's wide open door,
> The clouds wild trumpets blew,

Trees rose in wild dreams from the floor,
  Flowers with dream faces grew
Up to the sky, and softly hung
  Golden and white and blue.

. . . . .

The red deer of the forest dark,
  Whose antlers cut the sky,
That vanishes into the mirk
  And like a dream flits by,
And by an arrow slain at last
  Is but the wind's dark body.

The bull that stands in marshy lakes
  As motionless and still
As a dark rock butting from a plain
  Without a tree or hill;
The bull that is the sign of life,
  Its sombre, phallic will.

And from the dead, white eyes of them
  The wind springs up anew,
It blows upon the trembling heart,
  And bull and deer renew
Their flitting life in the dim past
  When that dead Hunter drew.

I sit beside him in the night,
  And, fingering his red stone,
I chase through endless forests dark
  Seeking that thing unknown,
That which is not red deer or bull,
  But which by them was shown:

By those stiff shapes in which he drew
  His soul's exalted cry,
When flying down the forest dark
  He slew and knew not why,
When he was filled with song, and strength
  Flowed to him from the sky.'

Another highly characteristic poem is 'Contemplation of Life.' The poet perceives in a vision that though life is mortal, yet Love is even more the prey of Death and has a shorter span.

'Upon a scene of endless transformation
I gazed unhappy, rivers came and faded,
Dragging a momentary brightness from the clouds
Into the monochrome of walling seas
Which leapt and fell with steady oscillation,
And in the crystal of eternity
Hung with a quivering wave-like repetition
The trees and mountains and the hollow valleys
With towns and peoples and a few fearful places
Where the soul *hunted* had leapt up and printed
On rock or tree or sheeted falling water
The sudden bright and diamond burning visage.'

Mr. Turner is, I hope, only at the beginning of his poetical career. It will be interesting to see if he ever amalgamates the two sides of his work—'Paris and Helen' and the black opal. I feel pretty hopeful that he will continue the mystical side of his work. It would be a great loss to modern poetry if he did not. The reader cannot help fancying that he has a good deal still to say.

VACHEL LINDSAY.

If ever there was a poet who even in these sophisticated days needed an interpreter, that poet is Mr. Vachel Lindsay. His mission is to take poetry out of the library; his poems are written for the enjoyment of the Plain Man. In America, where the Plain Man has less definite views of the proper habitat of poetry, it is immensely enjoyed. Possibly, unless its nature is a little explained, the Plain Man in England may regard it as not so much emancipated from the library as escaped from the menagerie.

But I don't think that when we come to consider his poems in detail we shall find them unduly alarming, unless we are over-obsessed by ideas about the dignity of literature, and we have forgotten Bacchus and Dionysus and our childhood. It is a pity to let the reading of Mr. Vachel Lindsay's poems make us feel scared and prim. For once, before the years had made us shy, there was a time when, in the right mood, we should have revelled in them—over the fire of an evening, or dabbling bare feet in a rock pool at the seaside. Then their high spirits, their enthusiasm, their 'guts and glow,' would have intoxicated us as they are meant to. Mr. Vachel Lindsay is a poet who speaks to our moods of freedom, to moods when we are away from hostile criticism, when, most of all, we are away from the odious spoil-sport who lives within us all, and whose acid 'You are making a fool of yourself' has made drab the lives of some of us for good and all. Those who have had the good fortune to hear Mr. Vachel Lindsay recite 'The Congo' will realise how much for its proper enjoyment it demands a certain abandon, an 'out of school' feeling, which for the self-conscious is only obtained in solitude or in carefully chosen society:

'Fat black bucks in a wine-barrel room,
Barrel-house kings, with feet unstable,

Sagged and reeled and pounded on the table,
Pounded on the table,
Beat an empty barrel with the handle of a broom,
Hard as they were able,
Boom, boom, BOOM,
With a silk umbrella and the handle of a broom,
Boomlay, boomlay, boomlay, BOOM.
THEN I had religion, THEN I had a vision.
I could not turn from their revel in derision.
THEN I SAW THE CONGO, CREEPING THROUGH THE BLACK,
CUTTING THROUGH THE FOREST WITH A GOLDEN TRACK.
Then along that riverbank
A thousand miles
Tattooed cannibals danced in files;
Then I heard the boom of the blood-lust song
And a thigh-bone beating on a tin-pan gong.'

There was no doubt that if the listener accepted Mr. Vachel Lindsay's mood, his use of the grotesque and the uncanny, there was something extraordinarily stirring and impressive about this passage as he chanted it. These opening lines are followed by an enlargement of the uncanny *motif*:—

'Death is an Elephant,
Torch-eyed and horrible,
Foam-flanked and terrible.'

Death is the servant of Mumbo-Jumbo, the ghost-god of the Congo,—Mumbo-Jumbo, god of secret and bloody rites. Then the mood of the poem changes, and at once we are confronted with the negroes in wild, childish high spirits. A 'Negro Fairyland' swings into view, where an ebony palace is guarded by a baboon butler, and the cake-walk princes laugh down the witch men who have threatened them with the dark terrors of Mumbo-Jumbo :—

> ' Just then from the doorway, as fat as shotes,
> Came the cake-walk princes in their long red coats,
> Canes with a brilliant lacquer shine,
> And tall silk hats that were red as wine,
> And they pranced with their butterfly partners there,
> Coal-black maidens with pearls in their hair;
> Knee-skirts trimmed with the jessamine sweet,
> And bells on their ankles and little black feet.'

They walk for a cake that is tall as a man, defiant of the witch men who finally are unable to resist the laughter and nonsense. But there is another side of the negro character. As a revivalist he can outdo Moody, Sankey, and General Booth. The old preacher

> ' Beat on the Bible till he wore it out
> Starting the jubilee revival shout.'

All along the valley of the Congo sweeps the cleansing fire of Christianity, sweeping over 'the vine-snared trees,' and the triumphant hymn goes :

> ' Mumbo-Jumbo will die in the jungle;
> Never again will he hoo-doo you,
> Never again will he hoo-doo you.'

. . . . . .

> ' Redeemed were the forests, the beasts and the men,
> And only the vulture dared again
> By the far, lone mountains of the moon
> To cry in the silence, the Congo tune :—
> " Mumbo-Jumbo will hoo-doo you,
> Mumbo-Jumbo will hoo-doo you.
> Mumbo . . . Jumbo . . . will . . . hoo-doo . . . you." '

The last lines are almost whispered.

When Mr. Vachel Lindsay repeats this poem himself it has a swing, a pageantry, and a glamour which are remarkable.

In nothing does Mr. Lindsay need the services of the critic more than in the matter of his stage directions. These are to be understood only by those to whom he has explained his theories of recitation, or rather as he prefers to call them, his 'habits.' When he recites he half sings and half speaks. The spoken parts are given with the orator's swing in a rhetorical passage; sometimes the swing is exaggerated till he is chanting. Now and then a lyrical piece will be crooned or sung to a simple musical tune of a few notes. All this may sound absurd, but I have had proof of this pudding and it is admirable. The method is all based on this theory: Mr. Lindsay thinks that poetry has lost a good deal by being written chiefly for the eye. On the other hand, he does not want to go back to the setting of poems to music, as he considers at the present day western music, even that written for the voice, has become so mathematical with its scales, tones and semi-tones, that it is too elaborate to be used merely to enhance the effect of the written word. There is another music of a more primitive kind which is much more to his purpose—that is, the music of the alphabet. A good French or English Actor, M. Coquelin or Mr. Henry Ainley, for instance, creates for any individual piece of blank verse or Alexandrine that he may be speaking, a beautiful pattern of sound, something which is almost a tune; something to which it is a pleasure for a foreigner to listen even if he cannot understand the words. This is the music which Mr. Lindsay seeks to develop, and it is with the accompaniment of a fairly elaborate voice pattern that his verse must be judged. The reader may object that it is no new thing to say that verse should be read aloud; this, of course, is perfectly true, but actually in practice both Mr. Lindsay's writing and delivery carry the process of good dramatic diction a little further. For instance, in the matter of writing, in each poem there are passages almost purely rhetorical, written in order that the speaker of them, the pattern-maker, may be able to convey a sense of, say, tranquillity or, on the other hand, of swift motion. For instance in 'The Santa-Fé Trail' the poet gives us a picture of a day spent under the arched sky of the wide Kansas Plain; he desires to give the reader a sense of the racing motor :—

> 'Butting through the delicate mists of the morning,
> It comes like lightning, goes past roaring '—

of the cars which stream all day out of the East towards the brown sea-sands of the Pacific coast :—

> 'Ho for the tear-horn, scare-horn, dare-horn,
> Ho for the *gay*-horn, *bark*-horn, *bay*-horn.
> *Ho for the Kansas, land that restores us*
> *When houses choke us, and great books bore us!*
> *Sunrise Kansas, harvester's Kansas,*
> *A million men have found you before us.*'

The first lines of this are, of course, simply syllables which, when properly spoken, will give a sense of swiftness and hurry. In their place they are effective and graphic.

It is very interesting to notice the effect of Mr. Lindsay's poems on the poetically unsophisticated. They prove a delight to the perfectly natural person or to the child. The mixture of humour, nonsense, and rhetoric, the high spirits, the go of them, act like wine when the listener is entirely unselfconscious and unprejudiced. It is for the unselfconscious and unprejudiced that they are intended. Perhaps Mr. Vachel Lindsay is one of the first people to do really good aesthetic work which is intended for 'natural man.' It is not here a question of 'writing down,' of words in one syllable, it is a question of appealing, as does Edward Lear's nonsense, to our simplest aesthetic tastes—the tastes which all of us share, but which have hitherto generally been appealed to so badly and so shabbily, that even the simple have been rather ashamed to acknowledge them and the sophisticated have suppressed them altogether as unworthy. It was not the tastes that were unworthy, it was the stuff that was provided for their satisfaction. Nor is the question of this satisfaction an academic or even a literary one; it is one which probably has more to do with human happiness than is as yet well understood.

MISS EDITH AND MESSRS. OSBERT AND SACHEVERELL SITWELL

If you go to see the glass-blowers of Murano they will sometimes give you little twisted blowings of glass that are like dolls or toy dogs. You used before the war to be able to buy this sort of toy, made a little more elaborately, in old-fashioned toyshops. They ended in a sort of spiral bit at ankles and wrists, they were very smooth, very bright in colour, very small and very brittle.

To the reader who comes unprepared upon the works of the Sitwell family the poems in 'Wheels,' 'the Wooden Pegasus,' and 'People's Palace' will seem to bear a strong resemblance to these dolls. For Messrs. Osbert and Sacheverell and Miss Edith Sitwell possess, besides the tastes and aims of more normal people, a genuinely fantastic imagination.

Those who dislike their poetry accuse them of being affected, they say that their oddity is nothing but a pose, that they are so effete that they can no longer enjoy the simple things of the world, and must have passed through a stage of mental debauchery thus to return to the childishness of a premature senility. All this sounds very plausible if we only read the parodies of their poems. It is easy and amusing to imitate their work, and we shall find successful imitations of their style in almost all the books of parodies that have appeared since the war. As a matter of fact, the explanation of their peculiarities is very much simpler than that. They possess, all three of them, unnaturally sharp sense perceptions and a habit of mind which is common with those who have such abnormally good eyes and ears. We see the same thing in Miss Dorothy Richardson's work. For purposes of expression, they translate sounds into sights and sights into sounds. Let me give a simple example, a frozen frost-rimed blade of grass is obviously a stiff; tense thing. Now tenseness translated into terms of sound would give the idea of high-pitch, and this is the mental process—not sheer devilry as some of her critics would hold—that makes Miss Sitwell in one of her poems speak of a blade of grass in the cold being 'shrill.' Further, as a family, they know a good deal about pictures, both ancient and modern, and so are very used to seeing the world through the eyes of a Tiepolo, a Paul Veronese, an El Greco, a Nevinson or an Ingres. This familiarity with the visual arts has very much increased what must be a natural tendency in them, a tendency to generalise what they see,—to see in patterns. Further a taste for satire and humour which is common to them makes them often see exceedingly funny patterns.

Here is a description of a piece of coast near Monte Carlo, by Mr. Osbert Sitwell :—

> 'Above from plaster-mountains,
> Wine-shadowed by the sea,
> Spurt white-wool clouds, as fountains
> Whirl from a rockery.
>
> . . . .

Through porous leaves the sun drops
  Each dripping stalactite
Of green. The chiselled tree-tops
  Seem cut from malachite.

Stiff leaves with ragged edges
  (Each one a wooden sword)
Are carved to prickly hedges,
  On which, with one accord

Their clockwork songs of calf-love
  Stout birds stop to recite,
From cages which the sun wove
  Of shade and latticed light.

Each brittle booth and joy-store
  Shines brightly. Below these
The ocean at a toy shore
  Yaps like a Pekinese.'

But Mr. Osbert Sitwell can be serious too. Here is the first verse of another poem; again he conceives in visual terms. The words are used chiefly for their roundness of sound and their beauty and colour :—

'Dusk floats up from the earth beneath,
Held in the arms of the evening wind
The evening wind that softly creeps
Along the jasper-terraces,
To bear with it
The old, sad scent
Of midsummer, of trees and flowers,
Whose bell-shaped blossoms, shaken, torn
By the rough fingers of the day
Ring out their frail and honeyed notes.'

Miss Edith Sitwell, with a slightly shorter range than her brother Osbert, has besides her satires, like him, written quite a number of 'straight' poems, many of them very successful. She is in her own style a poet whose works have extraordinary finish. She has always reminded me of a Vibrist painter. The adherents of this school have, beside a number of theories, one practice in common—they apply their paint in blobs. A grey is produced by innumerable definite specks of many bright colours so mingled as in totality to produce the effect of grey. As for the drawing, it is not done with lines, but is also done with blobs. Stand close to the picture, and it is generally impossible to gather the intentions of the painter either as to colour or form, but retire a little from it and the pattern becomes clear. Miss Edith Sitwell's work is like a Vibrist picture in being made up of innumerable small bright patches of colour—very clear, very bright, often startling, sometimes pretty. It is not everybody who can make little blobs of bright definite colour with printer's ink. To do so requires considerable artifice.

Take the following, which also contains some good instances of sense interchange :—

> 'Across the fields as green as spinach,
> Cropped as close as Time to Greenwich,
>
> Stands a high house; if at all,
> Spring comes like a Paisley shawl—
>
> Patternings meticulous
> And youthfully ridiculous.
>
> In each room the yellow sun
> Shakes like a canary, run

On run, roulade, and watery trill—
Yellow, meaningless, and shrill.

Face as white as any clock's,
Cased in parsley-dark curled locks.

All day long you sit and sew,
Stitch life down for fear it grow.

Stitch life down for fear we guess
At the hidden ugliness.

Dusty voice that throbs with heat,
Hoping with its steel-thin beat

To put stitches in my mind,
Make it tidy, make it kind;

You shall not! I'll keep it free
Though you turn earth, sky, and sea

To a patchwork quilt to keep
Your mind snug and warm in sleep.'

Another poem about trams in the same book (' The Wooden Pegasus,' a very apt title), is as gay and lively as a Lovat Fraser drawing :—

' Castles of crystal,
Castles of wood,
Moving on pulleys
Just as you should!
See the gay people
Flaunting like flags,
Bells in the steeple,
Sky all in rags' . . .

Miss Sitwell can also write seriously. The last poem in ' The Wooden Pegasus ' is on the theme of the man, who for the sake of a cruel wanton, murders his mother and is forgiven by her, the theme with which Mme. Yvette Gilbert used to make our hearts bleed with her whispered '*t'ai tu fait mal, mon enfant?*

Mr. Sacheverell Sitwell can write in the family satiric strain and write well, as, for example, in 'Mrs. H. . . or A Lady from Babel,' or he can write very charming 'straight' verse as in 'Serenade':

> 'Sigh softly, sigh softly,
> rain-thrilled leaves!
> Let not your careless hands
> Stem the gold wind!
> Let not your green sleeves
> Swim in its breath
> As water flowing!'

But he is a poet who very badly needs an annotator. The 'Lady from Babel' has been explained to me by one of his family, and directly we are put *en rapport* with it, is is obviously amusing and fulfils its light satirical purpose very well. Or take again 'Laughing Lions will come,' a very 'young' poem where, as in Mr. Vachel Lindsay's 'Golden Whales of California,' the poet oscillates between genuine and satirical gorgeousness. Here if the different portions of the poem are carefully marked off for us by someone who has got the key and it is explained to us exactly what the pieces of parody are intended to satirise, the poem becomes not merely not ridiculous (I confess to have felt sure it was ridiculous on first reading), but even moderately attractive.

Now for a poet to need annotation is not so much a proof of weakness in the poet, as a proof that there is something wrong somewhere. Who was it said that when we experienced the sensation of being bored we could only be sure of one thing—that there was a bore in company? So it is with this business of explanatory notes, either the reader or the poet is at fault. I used to be quite sure when a passage seemed obscure that it was Mr. Sacheverell who was in the wrong, but though I still tend to this opinion, I am by no means so sure of it as I was.

JOHN MASEFIELD.

Dr. Johnson declared that when we judged a poet we must grant him a certain amount of credit for the actual bulk of his work. It is impossible to consider the case of Mr. Masefield without believing that Johnson was to some extent right. There is no question here of promise and of hint. Mr. Masefield's poems unroll before us in a bright, many-coloured pageant of accomplishment.

He has plenty of faults. In every narrative that he has ever written there can be found (indeed there cry out) line upon line of mechanically contrived antithesis, line upon line of execrable phraseology. He is one of the easiest poets to parody; especially as he shows himself in the often crude thought and diction of the earlier poems. Mr. Masefield seems to have hardly any power of self-criticism, but will print the strangest piebald pieces of work. Take 'Enslaved,' for example; in the first seventeen pages, this poem ranges from the mediocre to the fantastically bad. This sort of beginning would, one would have thought have been enough to ruin any poem. Such loss in the attack must surely daunt any poet. Not at all! The whole of the rest of 'Enslaved' is in a different metre and in Mr. Masefield's most admirable narrative style. He is not a whit embarrassed or depressed. Quotation is almost impossible, for it is the quick breathlessness of the story and the anxiety we feel for the event which are so remarkable. His concern will not improbably make the reader miss much of the beauty of the verse at first perusal. The story, like an impatient guide, hurries us along at a running pace, and we only get a fleeting half-view of white toppling seas, of rigging black in the moonlight, of the dripping walls of a cave where the galley slaves are imprisoned, and of the high, white-washed walls of the Khalif's house of women at Marrakesh.

Mr. Masefield can always intrigue and excite his reader; he much more often makes a mistake in his capacity as a poet than as a story-teller, though, curiously enough, this instinct for plot and the arrangement of incident often deserts him when he turns to drama. There is a curious langour, for instance, about his 'Pompey the Great,' but this fault I think we can partly trace to the difficulty which I have tried to set out in speaking of Mr. Waley's Translations of the Japanese Nō Plays. Our convention is at the moment in a very uncomfortable state as far as the poetic drama is concerned. We have not yet found for it a form, a method of narration which will prevent the auditor pining for a realism which is rather beside the point in the poetic drama. In the case of Pompey the author vacillates too. I am not sure, though, that in one play Mr. Masefield has not got round the difficulty, and that is in 'Philip the King,' a one-act verse play of great merit, in which King Philip of Spain and the Infanta hear the news of the Armada, first a rumour of victory and then the truth. This, with its narration of physical events and our witnessing on the stage of the psychological effects of these physical events, seems to me to hit off very well the proper treatment of incident for a poetic play.

But people are perhaps too apt to consider Mr. Masefield only in his capacity as a writer of long narratives, the fact being that he can hold his own with most of his contempararies as a lyric and elegiac poet. For example, his beautifully polished and complete 'August, 1914,' is perhaps the best poem that the War produced. 'Biography' is another poem of extraordinary charm—simple, tranquil and extraordinarily individual and expressive. In the same volume as 'Enslaved,' there are also two exceedingly good ballads—'Cap on Head' and 'The Hounds of Hell.' The latter is one of the best poems of the Gothic Supernatural that has been writtence since 'Cristabel.'

Every night a ghostly huntsman, hunts living, sometimes human, prey over the Weald. Night after night the faint horn is heard, and some misfortune to flock or herd is discovered in the morning. At last a shepherd is found on the Downs with his throat torn, and no one dare any longer live in the haunted countryside:

> 'Men let the hay crop run to seed
> And the corn crop sprout in ear,
> And the root crop choke itself in weed,
> That hell-hound hunting year.'

At last St. Withiel, who lives not far thence, resolves that he will stop the powers of evil. He takes his stick and goes to this now desolated country where no human creature stirs. He will face the terror, whatever it may be. Night falls and all the powers of nature seem in league to terrify the saint:

> 'The darkness cackled in his heart
> The things of hell were there,
> That the startled rabbit played a part
> And the stoat's leap did prepare—
>
> Prepare the stage of night for blood,
> And the mind of night for death,
> For a spirit trembling in the mud
> In an agony for breath.'

At last, after an hour or two of such vigil, he hears, far away, the quavering death note blown on the devil's horn; another moment and he hears the hounds casting for him close at hand. They are in cry. Terror seizes him, he becomes a mere 'screaming will' to save his body from their jaws. He runs till his heart is ready to burst, and at last swings himself into a tree and so throws the hounds off for the moment. He hears them casting underneath him, ranging with softly padding feet. They are completely at fault, and at last the huntsman calls them off and silence falls again. Anguish at his failure seizes the saint. Christ died on a tree for him, but he has used a tree to hide. He comes down and resolves that he will dare the hounds again. But once more the cold note of the horn and the sound of the Hell Hounds on the scent turns his blood to water. This time, in his utter panic, the saint swims across a river and finds himself in a sort of paradise, and so fortified, has at last strength to go back to face Death and the Hounds, over whom he at last triumphs. Here is no botching work; every verse and every line is telling.

Mr. Masefield also knows how to write a sonnet. There is, for instance, a sonnet sequence called 'Animula' in 'Enslaved' that tells the story of a husband and wife, and of the lover with whom the wife will not fly. The woman, tormented by the love to which she will not submit and by her unhappiness with her suspicious, angry husband, seeks escape and throws herself into the sea:

> 'So, when the ninth wave drowned her, haply she
> Wakened, with merging senses, till she blent
> Into the joy and colour of the sea,
> One with the purpose of the element.
> And there, perhaps, she cannot feel the woe
> Passed in this rotting house, but runs like light
> Over the billows where the clippers go,
> One with the blue sea's pureness of delight;
> Laughing, perhaps at that old woe of hers
> Chained in the cage with fellow-prisoners.'

It is in such poems as this and the curious set of verses, called 'The Lemmings,' that the mystical element of Mr. Masefield's work is displayed. We realise something of the strength of this element in him when we consider how vivid is the extrovertic part of his nature. For outward things are never to him as we sometimes feel they are to Mr. Turner and Mr. Graves—valuable only in as far as they will serve as symbols by which it is possible to externalise and make tangible the adventures of the soul. Mr. Masefield is emphatically one who loves colours, sounds and sights for themselves.

It is perhaps in this power of caring for objects and events, both for themselves and as instruments shaping the mind of man, that Mr. Masefield's special strength lies. 'Reynard the Fox,' for instance, will please two sorts of reader or the same reader in two different moods. What we might call the two layers of its meaning have been treated with equal gusto by the poet. The result of this is that the poem is extremely vital and in a subtle sense —in spite of crude blemishes—harmonious. Soul and body are never at variance, neither has to drag a dead weight. It is perhaps in this remarkable integration, rather than in great force of intellect or fancy, that Mr. Masefield's strength lies. It may be that a good proportion of his faults occur in passages in which he has tried to alter the natural balance of the two elements.

WALTER DE LA MARE

PERHAPS no poet, except Shakespeare and Coleridge, has ever written such good magic poetry as Mr. de la Mare. There are, of course, a great many different sorts of magic poetry. There is the intimate bucolic rustic sort—Lobb and Puck bobbing for apples—there is the grand architectural sort, of which Coleridge was a master:

> 'But oh! that deep romantic chasm which slanted
> Down the green hill athwart a cedarn cover!
> A savage place! as holy and enchanted
> As e'er beneath a waning moon was haunted
> By woman wailing for her demon-lover!'

Or there is the arid horror of the witches in 'Macbeth' and the horses that 'eat each other.' But Shakespeare could do all kinds of magic. He could write, 'Fear no more the heat of the sun,' or the extremely advanced and Georgian, 'When that I was and a little tiny boy,' both of which belong to a very different kind of enchantment. Mr. de la Mare's magic is, as a rule, of this last type. We can parallel his prevailing mood in 'Full Fathom Five' or 'Come unto these yellow sands.' His work has the same remote, passionless beauty:

> 'Not a wave breaks,
> Not a bird calls,
> My heart, like a sea,
> Silent after a storm that hath died,
> Sleeps within me.

All the night's dews,
All the world's leaves,
All winter's snow
Seem with their quiet to have stilled in life's dream
All sorrowing now.'

Some people—the present writer confesses to have been long ago among them—find Mr. de la Mare's verse a little unsatisfying, a little too limpid, and inhuman. But now, since the 'collected edition' and the publication of 'The Veil,' his work can be considered in the mass. In some curious way, the short poems seem to reinforce one another and to create a remarkable atmosphere with their subtle cadences, the niceties of their rhythm and the extraordinary propriety of their vocabulary. These poems are like silk threads which are individually fragile, but which, woven together, make a fabric of unmatched fineness and strength, and one capable of taking on the softest, clearest colours. Here is one more example of this—Mr. de la Mare's main manner. It is 'The Sunken Garden,' perhaps after 'The Listeners,' his best-known poem:

'Speak not—whisper not;
Here bloweth thyme and bergamot;
Softly on the evening hour,
Secret herbs their spices shower,
Dark-spiked rosemary and myrrh,
Lean-stalked, purple lavender;
Hides within her bosom, too,
All her sorrows, bitter rue.

Breathe not—trespass not;
Of this green and darkling spot,
Latticed from the moon's beams,
Perchance a distant dreamer dreams;

Perchance upon its darkening air,
The unseen ghosts of children fare,
Faintly swinging, sway and sweep,
Like lovely sea-flowers in the deep;
While, unmoved, to watch and ward,
Amid its gloomed and daisied sward,
Stands with bowed and dewy head
That one little leaden Lad.'

But Mr. de la Mare has three other well-marked styles. I shall say nothing here of his poetry for children, except that I think that, on the whole, it is probably the best that has ever been written. Two of his most attractive essays in this vein are quoted on page 121 (Chapter 14). Then he knows another sort of magic. It must be a difficult kind to weave, because he seems only to bring off the spell occasionally. The magic is the evocation of one of Shakespeare's characters. Out of eight or ten attempts at materialisation, he twice produces the authentic personality. In 'Polonius' and 'Juliet's Nurse,' we feel sure—as Mr. Munro, I think, says somewhere—that Mr. de la Mare has got hold of some uncanny sort of private source of knowledge. How did he know just how, 'gloomy and wise and sly,' Juliet's nurse sat on in the old deserted nursery, gossipping to a young cousin from the country.

'There's not a soldier but hath babes in view;
There's not on earth what minds not of the midwife.'

Her mind is an anthill, and those eyes, 'arch, lewd and pious,' that know so effectively how to 'paint disaster with uplifted whites'! And those fat, small hands, 'babied hands' that pleat up or smooth the dark, handsome silk of her dress. How did he know?

What are Mr. de la Mare's faults? He has very few and they are not of great moment. First, I should put a tendency to use Thou and Thee without very sufficient reason, also he has a good many archaic words of which he seems rather over fond, such as 'groat,' 'helm,' 'wondrous,' even 'eftsoons.' Then some of his poems for children end sadly. That the instrument upon which he generally plays is a sort of poetic clavicord I hold to be no reproach. All art is to a great extent a process of limitation and selection. Mr. de la Mare's achievements more than justify him in the length to which he has carried this process. There remains, besides his rare 'vers de société,' one more manner to be considered. He has also written a few poems —there are three of them in 'The Veil'—which show a remarkable depth of human feeling. 'The Suicide' is one such poem, and another is 'The Dock':

'Pallid, mis-shapen he stands. The world's grimed thumb
Now hooked securely in his matted hair,
Has haled him struggling from his poisonous slum
And flung him mute as fish close-netted there.
His bloodless hands entalon that iron rail.
He gloats in beastlike trance. His settling eyes
From staring face to face rove on—and quail.
Justice for carrion pants; and these the flies.
Voice after voice in smooth impartial drone
Erects horrific in his darkening brain
A timber framework, where agape, alone
Bright life will kiss good-bye the cheek of Cain.

Sudden like wolf he cries: and sweats to see.
When howls man's soul, it howls inaudibly.'

Here speaks true compassion which knows that the innocent hold no monopoly of suffering.

If Mr. de la Mare does go on to develop this style, we shall see in his work a good example of the difference between Magic and Mysticism. Magic is mysticism externalised and personified. An elf or an apparition is a detached being, the personification of the oddness of some human creature. Therefore, the more oddness goes to the elf, and the more definite existence he has the less odd will be the human beings—actually and comparatively—with whom he is contrasted. The Mystic is like the pantheist, 'Lift the stone and I am there, gaze into the water, I am there.' The weaver of magic has in his personification taken the first step towards Olympianising the unknown.

All mystery gods, so Sir James Frazer tells us, become objective and Olympianised in time. This process, I fancy, we may be going to see reversed in the case of Mr. de la Mare's imaginings. 'The Veil' seems to contain indications that he is going to put the mystic element back into the very stuff of his poetry. The reader should consider the last two lines of 'The Dock' from this point of view.

ARTHUR WALEY.

Mr. Waley is a translator, but it would be as absurd to deny to him the title of poet as to refuse it to FitzGerald. Like FitzGerald he appears to be an interpretative artist of the finest sensibility, and—perhaps from his contact with a literature more delicate than the Persian—a metrical experimenter of the utmost skill. Though not announcing his theories in the matter of blank verse rhythms with the vigour of the imagists or of the disciples of polyphonic prose he has none the less perfected one or two beautiful unrhymed measures. Moreover, he has evolved a curious limpid crystalline vocabulary and style, its perfect transparence the result, the reader feels, in a high degree of the process of polishing. Here is an instance of Mr. Waley's method. The translation is from the works of Pö-Chu-i, and was written about A.D. 830. Pö-Chu-i, was, besides being a great poet, a high official, the humane and enlightened governor of a province:

' To a Talkative Guest.

The town visitor's easy talk flows in an endless stream;
The country host's quiet thoughts ramble timidly on.
" I beg you, Sir, do not tell me about things at Ch'ang-an,
For you entered just when my harp was tuned and lying balanced on my knees." '

But perhaps of an even higher quality is the following. Its eight lines surely express all the tragedy of slavery :—

'LOSING A SLAVE-GIRL.

Around my garden the little wall is low;
In the bailiff's lodge the lists are seldom checked.
I am ashamed to think we were not always kind;
I regret your labours, that will never be repaid.
The caged bird owes no allegiance;
The wind-tossed flower does not cling to the tree.

. . . . .

Where to-night she lies none can give us news;
Nor any knows, save the bright watching moon.'

Mr. Waley has also done another very interesting piece of work. He has translated and expounded a number of the traditional Nō Plays of Japan. Now these plays are chiefly interesting because they employ a very striking dramatic form. The time seems ripe in Europe for the revival of poetic drama. But at the moment the difficulty seems to be to hit upon a form in which we may crystallise our impulse.

For our poetic drama has certainly got to run concurrently with a realistic drama. Now the fault of the ordinary dramatic forms for the purposes of the poetic drama is that when a non-realistic drama is cast in these lines, however wild the plot, however improbable the characters, the audience unconsciously begin to miss the absent realism. In plays which are consciously archaic or even in the Elizabethan drama we are every now and then brought back to earth by our longing for realism. The music of Juliet's love lyrics is made a little unreal to us by speculations as to whether a young girl really would speak so, whether any passionate lover could find similes so exact, phrases so musical. The form adopted by the writers of the Nō plays is one so formal that it at once rids us of this difficulty. The plays are performed upon a stage divided into two parts, inner and outer. Ballet plays a considerable part in them. There are practically no properties and no scenery; the dress of the actors is, however, often magnificent, and certain of them are masked, and because there are no realistic properties the author need not hesitate to introduce into his drama boats, carriages, rocks, rivers, or trees as he pleases.

But the chief point of the form is that nearly all the action is both retrospective and yet at the same time of 'real' import at the moment.

There are too many ways of treating a theme according to Nō formulae for a summary here, but Mr. Waley gives all the necessary recipes in his preface, giving as an example the theme of the Duchess of Malfi treated in this way and reduced to two short acts.

EDWARD SHANKS.

I THINK if a lover of the classics came to me, or a man who read Milton, Keats and Wordsworth, and loved beauty and 'the grand style,' and told me that he desired to increase his range by an appreciation of modern poetry, and if he asked me how he had best approach it, I should give him Mr.

Edward Shanks' poetry to read. There are perhaps those who would say that in doing this I was not giving him modern poetry at all, that Mr. Shanks' work differs hardly perceptibly from the old tradition; but I think they would be wrong. Of course his methods perpetually remind us of 'the old masters.' There is a great deal of 'The Queen of China,' which reminds us, not perhaps of any particular Elizabethan, but of the general body of Elizabethan dramatic blank verse. Take the following, for instance:

'First Traveller: How stands the prince
In this new turmoil of the wildered court,
Who when we last were here was next the throne,
His father's chosen son?'

Chamberlain: He is grown grave.
Even as the king has waxed in youthfulness,
So he in gravity and the look of years.
You were his friends before, but you'll be fortuned
If now he will exchange five words with you.'

Or again, the following is unmistakably Miltonic:

Gobi and Shamo and the salten waste
Beyond Bokhara and the lonely marshes
That lie beside the desolate Caspian . . .'

'The Island of Youth' is full of echoes of Endymion, and here and there of Tennyson and Matthew Arnold. There is something as definitely Victorian in 'The Night Jars' as there is definitely Wordsworthian in the title, 'Stanzas Written in Dejection.' But Mr. Shanks is always using the old material for a new purpose, and that is why his poetry makes such a good introduction to modern verse for those brought up in the old tradition. He nearly always gives the content and purpose of modern verse, but he does not work with quite the usual Georgian means, and it is the means, not the end, that appear for the most part to frighten conservative lovers of verse.

If the reader expects me to tell him in so many words what the ends of modern poetry are, I am afraid he must be disappointed. If they could be stated in a sentence, it would not be necessary to take the great trouble of stating them in sonnets, epics or elegies. I am not sure that they are capable of direct statement at all. It must suffice to say here that they have something to do with human psychology. We are all conscious that there are elements within us—things in our outlook upon ourselves and the universe—which are highly elusive and difficult to express. The modern poet, like the seventeenth century metaphysical poet, finds himself for the most part engaged in an effort to show us some aspect or other of this irrational, but, as modern psychologists tell us, most real and most potent part of our make-up. Of course, all poets in all ages have tried to display man to himself, and the difference between, say, Donne and Tennyson, in this respect is one of emphasis. Both Donne and Tennyson were concerned with beauty, pattern-making, and the mind of man. Often Donne grew tired of his hard sayings and tried to express pure beauty : often Tennyson grew tired of beauty or didactic exposition and tried to express the inexpressible. But on the whole modern poets put the emphasis as Donne put it, and moreover use a medium a little like his methods of expression. Mr. Shanks, however, goes rather to the methods of Keats, Tennyson and Wordsworth. In unsuccessful lines, that is, he is apt to fall into such a phrase as:

> 'And long, long day added to long, long day
> In summer's fragrant count . . .'

But the general conception of 'The Island of Youth' is entirely modern. It tells the familiar story of how Thetis, by her enchantments, carried her son, Achilles, to Scyros, and there hid him disguised among the maidens of the island, and how, (the Oracle foretelling that the Greeks could not take Troy without Achilles' help) Ulysses was sent to find him out, which he did by means of a trick with a sword. Mr. Shanks has used the legend to convey a sense of the irrevocable fate of Man. Thetis has thought to cheat the Oracle, to cheat Death, but her son is mortal like the rest of us, and his fate cannot be gainsaid. The beginning of the poem is concerned with the sweet enchantment that Thetis—her son hidden—lays upon the island that has consented to be his asylum:

> '. . . . . . The simple island lords,
> Who ruled a land as peaceful as themselves,
> Careful to have the granges full of corn,
> The goat-skins plump with wine, the flocks and herds
> Guarded and tended to a due increase,
> Showed in their eyes, like a reflected light,
> Serenity, and in their bearing peace,
> And in their speech a cadence tranquiller
> Than they had used before. . . . .'

Sun, soft airs and a mild sea, prosper the affairs of Scyros as never before :

> ' And in that summer Thetis' blessing lay
> Especially upon her. Fishermen
> Thanked the sea-goddess for continual calm
> That lulled their storm-washed vessels near the rocks
> And herded in their nets the plenteous fish.
> The farmers watched their fields grow day by day
> More fruitful, and the vines under the sun
> More prosperously ripen to the vintage,
> Unvexed by creeping rot or summer tempest.
> Nor wolf nor murrain did the shepherd plague
> And on his thyme-grown hills he slept at night,
> Close by the dew-pond's green and glimmering round
> While all about him slept the peaceful flock
> Like white stones under the distant, kindly stars.'

The psychology of Achilles, whose whole nature has been changed to something of womanliness by his mother's spell, is delineated with a sure, light touch. The enchantment makes him unhappy, and uneasiness broods upon him. At last his hour comes. Ulysses' wile of the sword succeeds, not so much in revealing the truth to its deviser, as in teaching Achilles the truth about his own nature. He climbs up the hill-side and realises a future :

> ' Dark to forsee, but heavy with a sense
> Of weariness and blame and shame and tears.'

He throws aside his maiden's garments, and from that eclipse the hero's body rises ' sullen hued.' All night he wanders over the mountains and at last, sitting under an olive tree :

> ' Bowed his hot forehead into crampèd hands,
> Feeling a little world whose pulses beat
> Like earthquakes or annihilating wars.'

There are two very curious poems in the same volume—'The Emigration' and 'The End'—two poems which incidentally are much more modern in execution. One describes the weary trek of a whole people from a valley which their increasing numbers has made too narrow for their support. The other is a vision. In this the poet stands in a tangled wood and sees a rider on a rough, thin horse come slowly down an unused track. He is followed by a crowd of people—men and women of everyday, clerks, workmen and tramps, young girls, children, all the cavalcade of life; after them come beasts, all the homely animals that live about our houses. These in turn are followed by strange, unknown tropical creatures and strange birds that hover about the track. At last these too pass, and the poet sees with a sort of terror that the trees seem to be 'dragging their long roots' slowly out of the ground. The smaller plants follow like a swarm of bees, and the poet is left alone in a lifeless world. These two imaginings show Mr. Shanks in a somewhat new light, and when we take them in conjunction with the detachment and objectivity of such a poem as 'The Swimmers' and the gaiety of 'Fête Gallante,' we see what a wide range he possesses.

For 'Fête Gallante' is a lively piece of Versailles country sentiment. Aristonoë, the fading shepherdess, gathers the girls together—Celia, Rosalind, Phyllis, Helen and Chloe:

'Teaching them wisdom of love,
What to say, how to dress,

How frown, how smile,
How suitors to their dancing feet to bring,
How in mere walking to beguile,
What words cunningly said in what a way
Will draw man's busy fancy astray,
All the alphabet, grammar and syntax of Love.'

The garden is delicious and the high-heeled shoes print a turf starred with daisies. Some of the girls are not convinced that love is made of such crackling things as Aristonoë would have them believe:

'Celia tells the lesson over,
Counting on her fingers—one and two . . .
Ribbon and shoe,
Skirts, flowers, song, dancing, laughter, eyes,
Through the whole catalogue of formal gallantry,
And studious coquetries,
Counting to herself maliciously.'

There is yet another dress which Mr. Shanks wears with grace. He can write an admirable ballad:

'Oh, where are you, my own true love,
And why are you not here?
The nightingale amid the boughs
Is flattering his dear.

The night among the empty fields
Lies like a child at rest,
And empty, empty are my arms,
And light, too light, my breast.'

The verses which we have quoted surely witness to a very remarkable versatility, especially when we remember that the volume of 'The Queen of China' alone contains essays in three or four further distinct styles.

But though he shows versatility, Mr. Shanks shows curious faithfulness to poetic diction. He is quite content to let the cloud be 'the sun's first messenger,' he will say that a shell is 'rosy,' the ocean 'wild,' his storms are apt to 'prolong their turmoil.' Many modern poets would go miles to avoid such phrases, but Mr. Shanks' choice of them seems to me an interesting point in their favour, for he obviously does not use them ignorantly, though conceivably he may be a little too well read, and they may sing themselves to him so that he cannot avoid them. I do not think that is the case, however, for there are many poems in which he does so avoid them, but these are not poems into which we feel he has put his whole heart. 'Poetic language' seems to be his deliberate choice.

AMY LOWELL.

THE writings of Miss Amy Lowell are looked at rather askance in this country. This is perhaps not surprising: she has a vigorous assertive personality and a downright prose style, she is also rather apt to follow up dogmatic critical statements with weak lyrics written in accordance with her theories. Yet the theories are often ingenious. Sometimes the poems are not only weak, but prosy and academic, or even vulgar. In any case, in reading most of her verse, we are inclined to feel that, as a creative artist, the root of the matter is not in her. But in my opinion she has written one book which compensates for any number of failures. It is called 'Can Grande's Castle.'

Of course she must needs go and alienate half her readers by her preface! In it she seems to indicate that the 'polyphonic' or many-voiced prose in which she writes,—a free, elastic form, neither metrical, nor cadenced verse—is practically a new form which she has adapted from the French of M. Paul Fort. It is based, she says, upon the long flowing rhythms of oratorical prose. Really it *consists* of the long flowing cadences of oratorical prose! Now and then we have a bout of rhyming, but otherwise there is hardly anything of the book which, as far as manner is concerned, might not have been written by De Quincey, a forerunner whom she never mentions. This is not to decry 'Can Grande's Castle,' for Miss Lowell's work will easily bear comparison with his. De Quincey is often her equal in inspiration, but he had little except inspiration. The opium-eater had not energy left either for the sustained patterns or for the metaphysics of the American.

The second historical episode in the book tells the story of the forcible opening up of trade between America and Japan by Commodore Perry, who sails in the paddle-wheel frigate, 'The Mississippi' of the United States Navy. It is one of the best examples of her thought as apart from her form, one of the oblique descriptions of which she is so fond. (I guarantee that the passage makes capital good sense.)

'The Commodore writes in his cabin. Writes an account of what he has done. The sands of centuries run fast, one slides, and another, each falling into a smother of dust. A locomotive in pay for a Whistler; telegraph wires buying a revolution; weights and measures and Audubon's birds in exchange for fear. Yellow monkey-men leaping out of Pandora's box, shaking the rocks of the Western coastline. Golden California bartering panic for prints. The dressing-gowns of a continent won at the cost of security. Artists and philosophers lost in the hour-glass sand pouring through an open Gate.'

The reader must also be given a sample of her powers of description. Shall it be the account of the Carnival in decadent Venice? Shall it be of the great 'silver-white thunderheads' rising up over the rim of the sea off Aboukir Bay—Nelson going to fight the French? or shall it be Lady Hamilton? or the legionaries marching into Rome in the triumph of Titus? It is impossible to choose, but the book opens at the Roman incident. I accept the omen:—

'Morning in Rome; and the whole city foams out to meet it, seething, simmering, surging, sweeping. All between the Janiculum and the Palatine is undulating with people. Scarlet, violet, and purple togas pattern the mass of black and brown . . . What is that sound? The marble city shivers to the treading of feet. Cæsar's legions marching, foot—foot—hundreds, thousands of feet. They beat the ground, rounding each step double. Coming—coming—cohort after cohort, with brazen trumpets marking the time. One—two—one—two,—laurel-crowned each one of you, cactus-fibred, harsh as sand, grinding the rocks of a treeless land, rough and salt as a Dead Sea wind, only the fallen are left behind. Blood-red plumes, jarring to the footfalls; they have passed through the gate, they are in the walls of the mother city, of marble Rome. Their tunics are purple embroidered with gold, their armour clanks as they walk, the cold steel of their swords is chill in the sun, each is a hero, one by one, endless companies, the soldiers come. Back to Rome with a victor's spoils, with a victor's wreath on every head, and Judah broken is dead, dead! "*Io triumphe!*" The shout knocks and breaks upon the spears of the legionaries. The God of the Jews is overborne. He has failed his people. . . . Slowly they come, the symbols of a beaten religion: the Golden Table for the Shew-bread, the Silver Trumpets that sounded the Jubilee, the Seven-Branched Candlestick, the very Tables of the Law which Moses brought down from Mount Sinai. Can Jupiter conquer these? Slowly they pass, glinting in the sunlight, staring in the light of day, mocked and exhibited. Lord God of Hosts, fall upon these people, send your thunders upon them, hurl the lightnings of your wrath against this multitude, raze their marble city so that not one stone remain standing. But the sun shines unclouded, and the holy vessels pass onward through the Campus Martius, through the Circus Flamininus, up the Via Sacra to the Capitol.'

Then the refrain of the whole poem is repeated, the Motif of the Bronze horses of St. Mark's, a refrain that sounds through the din of the chariot-races of Constantinople; through the tinkling of the Carnival in Venice, through the tramp of Napoleon's armies of Italy.

'The bronze horses look into the brilliant sky, they trot slowly without moving, they advance slowly, one foot raised. There is always another step—one, and another. How many does not matter, so that each is taken.'

The passage I have quoted is surely an extraordinary *tour de force*, but it is a *tour de force* of which, in a hundred variations, Miss Lowell seems endlessly capable. The passages about Venice are as distinguished and appropriate as those which bring Rome before us :—

> 'Beautiful, faded city. The sea wind has dimmed your Oriental extravagance to an iris of rose, and amber, and lilac. . . . A tabernacle set in glass, an ivory ornament resting upon a table of polished steel. It is the surface of the sea, spangled, crinkled, engine-turned to whorls of blue and silver, ridged in waves of flower-green and gold.'

Has the reader noticed the interesting effect of the rhymes in the longest of the three passages quoted? Miss Lowell says in her preface that she is not yet satisfied that their printing as ordinary prose is satisfactory; in this I entirely agree with her. The effect is puzzling if an attempt is made to read the passages aloud, and this is, of course, the proper way to appreciate this type of *bravura* work.

'Can Grande's Castle' is an intoxicating piece of writing and deserves to be better known.

CHARLOTTE MEW.

THOSE whom we may, with only a little exaggeration call adherents of the 'Flat School' of Poetry have gained a great deal by their renunciation. Their effects are achieved by a great economy of language—literal as well as metaphorical, for their poems are generally short—by a certain metrical chastity, and by reliance on the poignancy of the commonplace if the object be narrative, and by the beauty of the ordinary if the object be landscape or symbolical.

Miss Charlotte Mew is of this school, and her work shows a wonderful degree of craftsmanship: we shall hardly ever find a word out of place or weak. She very rarely either uses an inversion or allows her rhyme to steer the course of her ship. Occasionally her emotion is exceedingly poignant, especially when she treats the idea—it recurs in several of the poems—of the dreamlike spell which hangs about the death of those we love or who are familiar to us. The raw grave, the broken fragment of a flower, cannot be the reality and the sense of continued companionship the illusion! A poem called 'Beside the Bed,' which is in some sense a complement of another entitled 'In Nunhead Cemetery' will give the reader some idea of her method:—

'Someone has shut the shining eyes, straightened and folded
The wandering hands quietly covering the unquiet breast:
So, smoothed and silenced you lie, like a child, not again to be questioned or scolded;
But, for you, not one of us believes that this is rest.

Not so to close the windows down can cloud and deaden
The blue beyond: or to screen the wavering flame subdue its breath:
Why, if I lay my cheek to your cheek, your grey lips, like dawn would quiver and redden,
Breaking into the old, odd smile at this fraud of death.'

Very often she writes as Crabbe might have written if he had been born in an age when free verse had loosed the bonds of narrative poetry; now and then as Pope might have written in the twentieth century.

There is a poem called 'Madeleine in Church' which reminds one of the passages from his 'Eloisa and Abelard':—

'Here, even, in this corner where my little candle shines
And overhead the lancet-window glows
With gold and crimsons you could almost drink
To know how jewels taste, just as I used to think
There was the scent in every red and yellow rose
Of all the sunsets.'

. . . .

'Oh! I know Virtue, and the peace it brings!
The temperate, well-worn smile
The one man gives you, when you are evermore his own:
And afterwards the child's, for a little while,
With its unknowing and all-seeing eyes
So soon to change, and make you feel how quick
The clock goes round. If one had learned the trick—
(How does one though?) Quite early on,
Of green pastures under placid skies,
One might be walking now with patient truth,
What did we care for it, who asked for youth,
When, oh! my God! this is going or has gone?'

The whole poem is a remarkable one, full of energy. Miss Mew seems to have caught exactly the point of view of the sort of woman she describes, and this is the more remarkable because in 'The Farmer's Bride,' the name-piece of her book, she has mastered and understood a very different type of sex-reaction in a woman. The farmer—we are given him in a few lines—a kind, busy, practical man, marries a very young girl who is as shy as a levret :—

> ' When us was wed she turned afraid
> Of love and me and all things human ;
> Like the shut of a winter's day.
> Her smile went out, and 'twasn't a woman—
> More like a frightened fay . . .'

But Miss Mew does not take up a conventional feminist ' gross male ' attitude. At the end of the poem she contrives to show us the affair from the farmer's point of view. The poem is full of humanity and sympathy. The Nemesis of Miss Mew's style is that she is apt to become prosaic. Very often the reader feels that her thought could have been more easily expressed in prose. But to those who value strength, poignancy, and economy her poems will always be interesting. Those who already admire her enough to study and re-read her verse are those who will find her most worthy to be admired. To say this is neither to praise nor to blame but to state a fact. For, though perhaps no good art is easy, yet poets should remember that beauty—in the narrow sense—remains the feather on the arrow, or the cheese in the mouse trap.

J. C. SQUIRE.

If, which heaven forbid! we had to characterise with a single word the mental attitudes of poets, that word in the case of Mr. Squire would certainly be detachment. Now, detachment is usually a secondary characteristic. It is caused by a quality in the mind for which we have no name in the intellectual sphere, but which in its social manifestation we call reserve or shyness. Some people seem to have a hedge about them which keeps them at a distance from their fellows and from direct contact with life. When they are men of intellect like Mr. Squire, and the quality is shown only in the sphere of some art, they are perhaps to be compared rather to men standing up on a little platform, such as is used by the umpire at lawn tennis or by the man who directs wanderers in the Maze at Hampton Court. Such writers are temperamentally onlookers, and we shall detect in their works the typical faults and virtues engendered by their position. Why such men find themselves on their little detached points of vantage I do not know, very often I think because of an unusual sensitiveness and an early realisation of men's follies and shortcomings. They shudder away from the stupidity and insensitiveness and vulgarity of such yahoos, and later, when wisdom has come to them, they are never quite able to make contact again. Such men obviously play a very valuable part. If they are poets or artists of any sort it is often they who acquire the greatest skill, for they are not detached because they don't feel strongly, but rather because they do. The difficulty comes in in the expression of their emotion. Their drums are apt to be muffled drums, and, realising how difficult it is going to be for them to express themselves, and passionately longing to do so, they are willing to go to great pains in acquiring skill for the attainment of their ends.

There will be another effect of this coolness and detachment. It will very often make for proficiency in a certain sort of humour—Mr. Squire, for instance, is perhaps the best living parodist—and it will often produce a fine reasoning and analytical critic. But the 'straight' expression of emotion is to such temperaments difficult. When they do succeed in breaking their bonds, however, we get something exceedingly beautiful, like Mr. Squire's 'You are My Sky.' We shall hardly, however, get anything bad from such a writer, for he will possess what his unconscious instinctive colleague will not possess—the power of self-criticism. He may possibly in secrecy write badly, but I doubt if he does, I doubt if he even thinks badly; the sloppy or the otherwise unworthy is nipped in the very smallest bud. Actually, Mr. Squire's sole lapse is, I think, 'The Lily of Malud.'

When Mr. Squire has a long poem in view how does he set about his work? Let us take for instance 'The Moon,' as perhaps being on the whole more typical than either 'Birds' or 'Rivers' and certainly than the 'Lily of Malud.'

Mr. Squire seems to have sat down to think all the things it is possible to think about the Moon and then determined to embody those thoughts in a form and style which would unify all the similes, epithets, sense-impressions, parallels and prophecies which had occurred to him. A reflective, low-toned elegaic note is sounded throughout the poem. The first stanza acquaints the reader with the atmosphere in which Mr. Squire proposes to make his effects :—

> 'I waited for a miracle to-night.
> Dim was the earth beneath a star-swept sky,
> Her boughs were vague in that phantasmal light,
> Her current rippled past invisibly.
> No stir was in the dark and windless meadows,
> Only the water, whispering in the shadows,
> That darkened nature lived did still proclaim.
> An hour I stood in that defeat of sight,
> Waiting, and then a sudden silver flame
> Burned in the eastern heaven, and she came.'

Mr. Squire has used his verse form with extraordinary accomplishment and subtlety. Every rhyme and assonance chimes upon the ear and gives that sense of roundness and completeness, that impression of a miniature refrain which (*pace* Milton, and Mr. Flint) is, after all, best produced by rhyme. The sense is carried on from stanza to stanza or from line to line just where it should be; it is broken when we feel the need of a pause. Mr. Squire twists words and rhythms as he will, the stubbornness they show in other hands has gone. The phraseology of the poem never startles the reader out of the tranquil mood that is to be evoked, and yet never allows him to sink into lethargy.

In many ways the poem is a pleasant and intended reminder of Young's, Thomson's or Cowper's elegaic style, especially, perhaps in the 'Last Man' *motif* at the end and the introduction of historical pieces in simile or in episode. The following verse, for instance, is an example of a more successful evocation of history than can be produced in what we may call the 'shrieks of an agonising king' style.

All our poor history, the poet says, has been unrolled before the calm eyes of Selene. Napoleon, alone in the night, felt rise above him :—

> 'The ancient conqueror's sloping, smooth, immense,
> Moon-pointing Pyramid's enduring courses.'
>
> . . . .
>
> 'Restless, he knew that moon who watched him muse,
> Had seen a restless Caesar brood on fame
> Amid the Pharoahs' broken avenues.
> And, circling round that fixed monition, came
> Woven by moonlight, random, transitory,
> Fragments of all the dim receding story :
> The moonlit water dripping from the oars
> Of triremes in the Bay of Syracuse ;
> The opposing bivouacs upon the shores,
> That knew dead Hector's and Achilles' wars.'

The poem concludes with an excellent 'end of the world' :—

> 'Pale satellite, old mistress of our fires,
> Who has seen so much and been so much to men,
> Symbol and goal of all our wild desires,
> Not any voice will cry upon thee then ;
> Dreamer and dream, they will have all gone over,
> The sick of heart, the singer and the lover,
> An end there will have been to all their lust,
> Their sorrow, and the sighing of their lyres ;
> O all this Life that stained Earth's patient crust,
> Time's dying breath will have blown away like dust.'

The poem, besides being a *tour de force* in its sustained unity, is exceedingly agreeable reading.

As we might expect from a poet who is also a scholar (almost a literary collector) Mr. Squire is often very good at half-historical, half-scientific effects. Take the following, for instance, from 'Birds':—

'Oh let your strong imagination turn
The great wheel backwards until Troy unburn,
And then unbuild and seven Troys below
Rise out of death and dwindle and outflow,
Till all have passed and none has yet been there.
Back, ever back.'

'A Far Place,' one or two of his songs, and 'To a Bulldog,' are some of the most attractive of Mr. Squire's poems, but personally I have as favourite the beautiful song 'You are my Sky':—

'You are my sky; beneath your circling kindness
My meadows all take in the light and grow;
Laugh with the joy you've given,
The joy you've given,
And open in a thousand buds, and blow.

But when you are sombre, sad, averse, forgetful,
Heavily veiled by clouds that brood with rain,
Dumbly I lie all shadowed,
I lie all shadowed,
And dumbly wait for you to shine again.'

But Mr. Squire is nothing if not an experimenter. His latest considerable poem is an account of the Oxford *v.* Cambridge Rugby Football match. The poem is a moment-to-moment diary of the sense perceptions and fleeting emotions of an on-looker at the match. It is written colloquially in an informal measure with occasional rhyming. Some of the best lines in the poem are about the crowd.

It might, by the way, be instructive to study the differences between Mr. Squire's and Mr. Masefield's treatment of the onlookers at a sporting event:

'Oh, Lord, ! What an awful crush ! There are faces pale
And strained, and faces with animal grins advancing,
Stuck fast around mine. We move, we pause again
For an age, then a forward wave and another stop.
The pressure might squeeze one flat. Dig heels into ground,
For this white and terrified woman whose male insists
Upon room to get back. Why didn't I come here at one?
Why come here at all? What strange little creatures we
 are,
Wedged and shoving under the contemptuous sky !

* * * * *

All things have stopped ; the time will never go by ;
We shall never get in ! . . . Yet through the standing glass
The sand imperceptibly drops, the inexorable laws
Of number work also here. . . .'

The reader notes the detachment. Mr. Squire does not in the least mind the accusation of being a moralising Jacques, and has in this poem written that which many modern poets would have been afraid to write and will be shy to read. This in my mind is a sign of strength in Mr. Squire, and of weakness in those who will be shocked. Very effective in the poem is the alternate sense in the narrator of identity with the crowd and of separation from it. The onset of the early winter twilight, with the air grown blue and misty and the players only seen dimly as they drift away to a distant corner, matches lit by men in the stands on the opposite side of the ground beginning to show up as little yellow spurts of flame—all this is admirably given, with its psychological consequences.

At the end of the poem I think Mr. Squire makes a mistake. He takes the implicit comment of the early part of the poem a step further, and gives us not the fragmentary fleeting thoughts which were so effective earlier, but a whole slab of comment. I think he should have left this to the reader's imagination and not stated it, for it was all sequestered in what he had written before. We should have got there all right, and now, by stating his comment in so many words, he has taken the fine edges off it; he has tried to state what is really an attitude of mind too plainly, and has foregone the magic of poetry which he had used fully in the earlier part of the poem—its power of expressing the inexpressible.

I wish space allowed me to draw the reader's attention more fully to the fascinating qualities of 'Winter Nighfall,' with its intriguing use of assonance, rhyme and repetition, or 'Meditation in Lamplight' (a good example of the category type of poem of which Mr. Squire is so fond), to the beautiful Chinese effects of 'Fen Landscape,' and to the perpetual delights of that most beautiful poem, 'A Far Place,'

EDMUND BLUNDEN.

Mr. Blunden seemed so far one of those poets who succeed largely by reason of their willingness to limit their province. He gives us a kind of poetic *Petite Culture*. No mixed farming for Mr. Blunden, he will not disperse himself here and there, but will get all he can out of his one carefully-dug patch. It would be almost possible to count Mr. Blunden's subjects (and his unsuccessful poems, too, be it noted) on the fingers of one hand. His work is singularly direct. His landscape is that of Kent and Sussex. Hops, mill-ponds, oast-houses, streams, and, above all, fish are his themes, and he almost invariably manages to make his readers visualise these objects as he desires.

> 'The wild-rose bush lets loll
> Her sweet-breathed petals on the pearl-smooth pool,
> The bream-pool overshadowed with the cool
> Of oaks where myriad mumbling wings patrol.
>
> . . . . . .
>
> Up the slow stream the immemorial bream
> (For when had Death dominion over them?)
> Through green pavilions of ghost leaf and stem,
> A conclave of blue shadows in a dream,
> Glide on; idola that forgotten plan,
> Incomparably wise, the doom of man.'

Such is the note of most of his poems; it is struck with a sure, full chime in Almswomen. He describes how two old women love and depend upon one another, 'like true loves in the spring.'

'Long, long ago they passed threescore-and-ten,
And in this doll's house lived together then;
All things they have in common, being so poor,

. . . .

How happy go the rich fair-weather days
When on the roadside folk stare in amaze
At such a honeycomb of fruit and flowers
As mellows round their threshold; what long hours
They gloat upon their steepling hollyhocks,
Bee's balsams, feathery southernwood, and stocks.'

More rarely, but with as sure a touch, he evokes a mood, as in Sickbed or in Leisure, where he writes:

'Of autumn half-asleep and idly playing
With fancies as they chance,
The feather's fall, the doomed red leaf delaying,
And all the tiny circumstance of peace.'

Lately, however—notably in Oxford Poetry, 1921—he shows signs of extending his range and subject. Before Mr. Blunden writes perfectly of his bit of country and grows a complete interpreter, he must do what he seems to be striving for—catch a little more of the wantonness, the caprice, the wildness, that storm, sunrise, and moonset give even to the quietest country-sides. He must persevere and develop the vein of waywardness that is now nearly hidden. He has at present too much of the Thomson—the Correct Pastoral attitude. He might at any moment lapse into the gentlemanly naturalist, the reader feels. We almost expect some phrase of 'the market-place o'erspread with poor.' Here is soil from which smugness might grow; we miss a sub-acidity, a tartness.

This, however, is to cavil. It is not fair to commend Mr. Blunden for concentration and then blame him for lack of diversity. And within his self-imposed boundaries his work is satisfying, and vigorously simple. Mr. Blunden is not only a writer of a very high order of talent, he is a poet, a man whose work illumines and interprets that of which he writes, even to those who seemed to know it best.

JAMES ELROY FLECKER.

JAMES Elroy Flecker was what we might call an early-modern. Superficially, or at any rate technically, he did not depart very far from the Victorian tradition. In style his chief divergence was one of diction, while in metre and construction he often equals the Victorians in elaboration and surpassed them in subtlety. Even in diction the changes he made were of omission. He denied himself on the one hand those 'poetic' words which his predecessor had overworked, and on the other the many markedly prosaic expressions with which his successors have made us familiar in poetry. His 'Ballad of the Londoner' may stand as an example of his use of words—though indeed it is also typical of his work in a wider sense.

> 'Evening falls on the smoky walls,
> And the railings drip with rain,
> And I will cross the old river
> To see my girl again.

The great and solemn-gliding tram,
  Love's still mysterious car,
Has many a light of gold and white,
  And a single dark red star.

I know a garden in a street
  Which no one ever knew;
I know a rose beyond the Thames,
  Where flowers are pale and few.'

In some respects how perfectly classical this is—how consonant with tradition! Indeed, the last two lines are so almost comically Wordsworthian that we feel the lady's name can only have been Lucy. And yet could anyone mistake this for anything but a modern poem? As to Flecker's use of unpoetic objects and images—in this case the tram—it is easy to see, but hard to define how his lines differ from what Mr. Huxley on the one hand, or Swinburne on the other, would have written. Perhaps we notice, first of all, that Flecker is obviously deeply interested in what a tram at night is really like, its pictorial effect, and in a brilliant line he gives it:

'The great and solemn-gliding tram.'

But Flecker is a transitional, and he is therefore self-conscious about his tram, and so tries to prove its fitness to figure in a poem by calling it 'Love's still mysterious car.' He is in fact still challenging the people who see a tram, not as a fact, but as a street nuisance, or *per contra*, as a democratic public conveyance. But then his pictorial interest reasserts itself and again one sees the wet sheen of the streets:

> 'Has many a light of gold and white
> And a single dark red star.'

But perhaps the boundaries of his interest are even more significant. It is evidently no concern of his whether the tram does good or harm. A Victorian poet would have felt much less interest in what the tram looked like than in his own conception of it as:

(1) A car of Juggernaut defiling God's beautiful earth, or:

(2) The triumphant symbol of democracy.

Yet Flecker's reaction to the tram would not be in the least that of one of the younger poets of the present day—Mr. Golding, Mr. Rickward, Mr. Hughes, Mr. Porter—they would never have put in that line of apology, 'Love's still mysterious car,' any more than they would write the internal rhyme in the first line. Consider, for example, the perfect *sang froid* with which Miss Edith Sitwell writes about trams. But fortunately, the fact of standing between two conventions never seriously hampered Flecker. His genius was bold and copious, and strong enough to sweep aside technical difficulties that would have strangled a lesser man. Above all, Flecker was one of those beings who seem to possess a peculiar power over words. It is arguable that he did not understand life or psychology as well as his successors or his critics, but he understood the art of writing much more profoundly.

Perhaps I can best illustrate his power over words by quoting from one of his early poems, 'The Bridge of Fire.' It is a poem easy to criticise for its looseness of construction, its lack of overt meaning, and it is not, of course, to be compared to his mature work.

In this poem we seem to see a young mind turning over and caressing the rich and glorious jewels of antiquity and tradition. Here are the materials with which he will presently build. But for the present he is content to let them run through his fingers. He sees the Gods on Heaven's Bridge:

'Robed with faint seas and crowned with quiet stars
All great Gods dwell to whom men prayed or pray.
No winter chills, no fear or fever mars
Their grand and timeless hours of pomp and play;
Some drive about the Rim wind-golden cars
Or, shouting, laugh Eternity away.
    The daughters of their pride,
    Moon-pale, blue-water-eyed,
Their flame-white bodies pearled with falling spray,
    Send all their dark hair streaming
    Down where the worlds lie gleaming, . . .'

He tells of the Greek Gods:

'The Gods whose faces are the morning light,
Of they who love the leafy rood of song,
The Gods of Greece, dividing the broad night,
Have gathered on the Bridge, of all that throng
The fairest, whether he whose feet for flight
Had plumy wings, or she to whom belong
Shadows, Persephone, or that swan-white
Rose-breasted island lady, gentle and strong, . . .'

But there are darker Gods:

'Belus and Ra and that most jealous Lord
Who ruled the hosts of Pharoah in the sea, . . .'

. . . . . .

'Gods who take vengeance, gods who grant reward,
Gods who exact a murdered devotee,
Brahma the kind, and Siva the abhorred
And they who tend Ygdrasil, the big tree,
And Isis, the young moon,
And she of the piping tune,
Her Phrygian sister, cruel Cybele,
And Orpheus the lone harp-player
And Mithras the man-slayer,
And Allah rumbling on to victory,
And some, the oldest of them all,
Square heads that leer and lust, and lizard shapes that crawl.'

Though perhaps we ought to deny to this the title of 'great poetry,' because it has neither deep emotion or particularly profound thought behind it, we must yet admit that it is, like the more mature 'Pillage,' the most gorgeous word magic. I suppose 'Pillage' is the most highly-finished and highly-polished piece of decorative writing that the modern movement has given us. Few of us who have fallen under its spell will forget the sense of intoxication that first reading brought with it. Here is the last verse:

'No more when the trumpeter calls shall we feast in the white-light halls;
For stayed are the soft footfalls of the moon-browed bearers of wine,

And lost are the statues of Kings and of Gods with great glorious wings,
And an empire of beautiful things, and the lips of the love who was mine.'

But perhaps more lasting, because perhaps more subtle, are the opening lines of 'Sanţorin,' one of the few pieces of free verse that Flecker wrote:

> 'Who are you, Sea Lady,
> And where in the seas are we?
> I have too long been steering
> By the flashes in your eyes.
> Why drops the moonlight through my heart,
> And why so quietly
> Go the great engines of my boat
> As if their souls were free?'

Our wonder at the sense of glamour it has evoked will perhaps be succeeded by surprise at the extraordinary impression of smoothness which so free a measure has been made to give us. It is easy enough, of course, to see where the rhymes occur, but they seem to be introduced according to no regular scheme; there appears to be no fixed cadence (compare the lines I have quoted of Miss Amy Lowell's 'Patterns'), there seems to be no fixed plan in the length of the lines and the numbers of the syllables. It is, I think, a poem which we might very well adduce as a proof of the truth of some of the allegations that I made in the chapter on Metre and Prosody.

I must in conclusion warn the new reader that he must not form an opinion of Flecker's poems from the fragments I have quoted. Flecker, much more than his successors, wrote his poems as wholes, and to take an extract is usually an act of violence.

I hope, at any rate, that I have shown that Flecker was not, as has sometimes been said, the poet with the modern content and the Victorian manner. Perhaps his detachment is one of his most marked characteristics. He excluded with wonderful success all that had become impossible, that had been worked to death in the Victorian method, and yet wasted no time in 'breaking with tradition,' being so sure of himself that he could pass straight to creation, clear in his individuality, fearing neither the old nor the new. I think that his reputation will grow with the years as Keats' reputation—probably even smaller at the time of his death than Flecker's—grew, until they will both be secure in the possession of all those minds which can love the sheer beauty of words and word-images for their own sakes, and without an *arrière pensée* of regret for an absent psychological revelation.

RUPERT BROOKE

RUPERT Brooke was certainly at one time the most discussed poet of the modern movement. A romantic and untimely death cut him off from what promised to be a sustained productiveness, and every poem of his lamentably small output has been thoroughly considered and commented upon—turned this way and that—by poets and critics.

Unlike that of the majority of modern poets, Brooke's reputation has suffered from a good deal of rather uncritical admiration, than which there can be nothing more damaging, and consequently at the moment there is perhaps a tendency to underestimate his great powers and his greater promise.

For in spite of his scholarship and his remarkable acomplishment as a versifier, immaturity seems to me the outstanding characteristic of Brooke's work. His was probably one of those minds and certainly one of those characters which mature late. Not only too was he personally young, but his work was the product of the extreme youth of a movement. Brooke had neither personal nor traditional roots. We feel all the time that he is making an effort to keep his balance. There is hardly a poem of his which does not show, as well as the charm, the self-consciousness of immaturity:

'Hot through Troy's ruin Menelaus broke
To Priam's palace sword in hand, to sate
On that adulterous whore a ten years' hate
And a king's honour. Through red death and smoke,
And cries, and then by quieter ways he strode,
Till the still innermost chambers fronted him.
He swung his sword, and crashed into the dim
Luxurious bower, flaming like a god.

High sat white Helen, lonely and serene,
He had not remembered that she was so fair,
And that her neck curved down in such a way;
And he felt tired. He flung the sword away,
And kissed her feet, and knelt before her there,
The perfect Knight before the perfect Queen.'

The choice of such a subject was vain, the poet has

no more got away from himself than he did in 'Granchester' or 'Channel Crossing.'

Now self-consciousness in the poet is very apt to have much the same effect upon the reader as has shyness in an interlocutor. In some subtle way it makes us not only restless and uncomfortable, but unduly critical. The poet, we feel, is being self-assertive and mannered and, though we know it is from fright, it has its effect nevertheless. However, the fault luckily by no means spreads itself over Brooke's entire output. For instance, though the self-consciousness is there, it does not obtrude itself in what I consider to be one of Brooke's most delightful poems, 'Dining Room Tea.'

A party of intimates are sitting at tea, laughing and talking. Suddenly the poet experiences a sensation of *isolment*, a sensation with which we are all of us probably familiar in some form. The whole scene suddenly becomes static, and at the same time he becomes aware of a sort of inner meaning in it all. What this inner meaning may be he naturally does not state; that would be impossible, it can only be apprehended by a mind illuminated by the vision :

> 'I saw the marble cup; the tea,
> Hung on the air, an amber stream;
> I saw the fire's unglittering gleam,
> The painted flame, the frozen smoke.
> No more the flooding lamplight broke
> On flying eyes and lips and hair;
> But lay, but slept unbroken there,

On stiller flesh, and body breathless,
And lips and laughter swayed and deathless,
And words on which no silence grew.
Light was more alive than you.'

Alas! that Brooke did not live so that his force might have grown into strength, his irritability into humour, his irony into wit, his charm into a majestic beauty. Everything in the turn that the poetic movement has taken would have served to ripen and mature Brooke's genius.

ROBERT NICHOLS.

Mr .Robert Nichols' virtues are many. Oftener than his reader has a right to expect—for every poet has a fixed allowance of failures per successful set of verses—he achieves limpidity, perfect poetic fusion. In a great deal of the poetry that we are quite ready to enjoy, the thought and the medium remain as it were distinct. Throw a pinch of salt into a tumbler of water, and for a moment the grains sink visibly; there is salt, there is water, but in another moment there is salt-water. Mr. Nichols' 'The Sprig of Lime' and 'Night Rhapsody' are salt water. They and some fragments of other poems approach perfection. Therefore it is that Mr. Nichols' work must be judged by absolute standards. When a poet has attained to a certain mastery, we can no longer soothe our aesthetic consciences by saying that his work is marvellously good for, say, a first-lieutenant or a bombardier, excuses with which the critic—sated with blood—is apt to disguise the lenient judgments of laziness. We must begin to ask ourselves why each particular poem misses perfection. We must inquire why, though we read and re-read an individual poem, the grains are still visible; we must ask what quality is it that keeps them in suspension.

What are Mr. Nichols' faults? They are many and diverse. Sometimes the difficulty is that his grains of salt belong to somebody else. For example, in 'The Deliverer,' as they sink down to the bottom of the tumbler, they spell 'John Masefield' and 'Lascelles Abercrombie.' In the sixteenth sonnet to Aurelia, the legend is 'Rupert Brooke.' There has been very little assimilation. We can find the very sonnet, 'Helen and Menelaus II':

> 'And you poor drivelling, disregarded crone,
> Bide blinking at memory between drowsy fits.'
>
> . . . . . .
>
> 'Oft she weeps, gummy-eyed and impotent.'

A different fault is his ability to write slovenly verse. For example, in 'Two Friends, Two Nights,' the thought is a sound one, but it has not been hammered out. Mr. Nichols has been content with a poem before it was half forged. The fault is not in individual lines, but in conception. Perhaps the key to this trouble lies in a certain vanity, a certain egotism which Mr. Nichols displays naïvely enough in some of his poems. Every now and then he produces the impression of flinging a piece of work at the reader and saying, 'This is a poem by Robert Nichols; read and be thankful.' It is a fault of taste, for it is arguable that no one human being is much more egotistical than another; merely some men have skill enough to hide the long ears of our common nature.

Lastly, he has too little sense of humour, that last fairest blossom of a sense of proportion. Satire in his hands might, the reader imagines, become invective—it would never become banter. It might be terrible, but it would not be amusing.

But all these are the faults of youth, and, with some of its faults, Mr. Nichols has all of its virtues. He is adaptable, he is resourceful, he is restlessly eager to try new methods, to pour his soul into an unaccustomed vessel. He has force, eloquence, fire, and passion, and he has a *terribilità* which will remind the reader of Donne, in whose work Mr. Nichols has obviously steeped himself, though he does not imitate him.

He has considerable power of characterisation. For example, the charming conversation between the poet and his friend, Mr. Robert Graves, called 'Winter Overnight.'

Very different, again, is 'The Flower of Flame,' in the first two verses of which we have—to pursue our original analogy—another salt-water poem, one in which fusion is perfect:

> 'As round the cliff I came alone
> The whole bay bared its blaze to me;
> Loud sung the wind, the wild sun shone,
> The tumbled clouds fled scattering on,
> Light shattered on wave and winking stone.'

'The Sprig of Lime' was among the first of his reflective poems. Perhaps some readers may feel that the later 'Night Rhapsody' is almost more exquisite :

> 'How beautiful it is to wake at night,
> When over all there reigns the ultimate spell
> Of complete silence, darkness absolute,
> To feel the world, tilted on axle-tree,
> In slow gyration, with no sensible sound,
> Unless to ears of unimagined beings,
> Resident incorporeal or stretched
> In vigilance of ecstasy among
> Ethereal paths and the celestial maze.
> The rumour of our onward course now brings
> A steady rustle, as of some strange ship
> Darkling with soundless sail all set and amply filled
> By volume of an ever-constant air,
> At fullest night, through seas for ever calm,
> Swept lovely and unknown for ever on.
>
> . . . . . .
>
> How beautiful to wake at night,
> Within the room grown strange, and still, and sweet,
> And live a century, while in the dark
> The dripping wheel of silence slowly turns.'

There never lived a poet who would not have been proud to have written such lines. They have achieved completeness, they have an independent life of their own.

INDEX

Titles of Poems and Books are in italics.

V

W

Y

HOLYWELL PRESS, ALFRED STREET, OXFORD.

CPSIA information can be obtained
at www.ICGtesting.com
Printed in the USA
BVHW031019150819
555975BV00002B/263/P

9 789353 808440